REDEFINING YOU

REDEFINING YOU

Radical Transformation Strategies for
Development from Within

Enakeno Victoria Oju

Redefining You. © 2019 Enakeno Victoria Oju. All rights reserved.

No part of this book may be reproduced, stored in a retrieval system, or transmitted by any means without the written permission of the author.

Published by Revicena Int'l Ltd—24/05/2019

Cover Designed by Adeleye Sodade
Cover Photo by Pro Church Media on Unsplash

ISBN: 978-978-57022-0-0

DEDICATION

This book is dedicated to everyone out there who wants to transit from being powerless, vulnerable, invisible and scared to being, Strong, Confident, Independent and Relevant

CONTENTS

	Acknowledgments	i
1	Introduction	1
2	What's in Your Way?	5
3	Who Are You	9
4	Fundamentals	13
5	The Transformative Process	19
6	Decisions	25
7	Setting Your Goals	33
8	On Your Journey	39
9	Some Fruits of Your Efforts	47
10	Vital To Your Success	61
11	Association	75
12	Some Truths About Your Journey	83
13	More Truths About Your Journey	99
14	Still More Things to Do	111
15	Conclusion	119
	Afterword	123
	Checklists	125

ACKNOWLEDGMENTS

I will like to acknowledge a couple of people who are always there for me:
my parents Simon and Theresa Oju; my twin sister, Vivien Ekamah; my cute younger sister Fuafo-Eleanor; my brothers – Rex, Evi, Ono's and Zito; my nieces – Emmanuela, Vivien Jnr and Onah.
Your love and support mean so much to me.

I also want to thank my dear friend Africa for his contribution.

And to Sandra, *I will always be grateful to you for the vital role you continue to play in my career trajectory.*

1

INTRODUCTION

Radical Woman! Radical Woman!! The Radical Woman!!! This idea just kept haunting me for a couple of weeks. Anywhere I turned; the word *Radica*l kept coming back to me. The Radical Woman! Who she is! Who she is not! These were the thoughts that preoccupied my entire mind for a while before I began writing this book.

Certainly, the *Radical Woman* creates her own reality and the life of her dreams.

It took me a long while to begin to create my own reality and now, I feel this compelling urge to share with you what I've learned. I couldn't find peace within me until I put on my PC and started writing.

What Do I Want to Do Here?

I want to help people who are feeling stagnant in certain areas of their lives; who are dissatisfied with their life like I was at some point.

Until recently, I spent my days figuring out why I'm here and how to get from where I am to where I want to be. It took me years of hard work and a lot of heartbreaks plus countless trial and errors with mistakes to finally figure out what matters and how to manifest my desired reality. Anyone who is at that place that I was until recently, you are in the right place.

Whenever you are feeling stuck as you navigate your journey in life, it's a sign. It's a signal that your fundamental need for growth and exploration is not being met. In other words, you are not making progress and living up to your highest potential, therefore not living the life of your dreams. This book presents radical transformation tools that will help you get out of your way, take action and achieve the life you dream of.

Our life is our biggest design project; we need to give it our best shot now. This is the only chance we've got; there is no second run.

This book is for you if:
- You want to have a high level of respect for yourself and be respected by others
- You want to love and be loved genuinely
- You want to be relevant
- You want to get ahead
- You want to be happy in your work
- You want to be successful
- You want to experience true power
- You hunger for better things but don't know how to begin
- You are tired of being invisible
- You want to move from passive mode to active mode
- You want to be wealthy
- You want to have amazing and quality relationships
- You want to increase your influence
- You want to be free from most anxiety
- You want to be free to do what you want, when, where and how
- You want to help make the World a better place

I am a Man, and I am Reading this Book

Thank you for picking up this book. The principles presented in this book are universal and will work for anyone regardless of age, gender and race; they will be of great help to you in redefining your life and changing the trajectory of your life.

I am a Woman, and I am Reading this Book

This book presents some basic skills that will help any woman stand on her feet. No matter what age and where she is starting. She is presented with the skills to tackle anything life throws at her and how to achieve success and get anything she wants.

It's about time women all over the world woke up from the laid back position where they expect to receive, receive and receive only without making efforts to give or contribute to overall development. Women, have the potentials to become *trendsetters* instead of trying to be like others and living in the shadows of others. I have set some myself before in my environment, and it wasn't rocket science at all. All I did was follow my instincts, not minding what others thought or didn't think.

You can not be a radical woman and not be a success. As a radical and revolutionary woman, you excel in everything you do. And with success, comes power, wealth, fame and quality relationships. You won't look for them; they will look for you.

What gives me the authority to ask you to follow the principles in this book?

It's about time you asked I guess. I'm not writing because I'm perfect. I'm far from it. I write because these concepts and ideas have helped me transform my life and I want you to learn them too.

Everything I am set to share with you here has been tested and proven in the crucible of real life. Following these steps changed my life immensely and the lives of a whole lot of other people. I grew from one insecure little girl who felt powerless and accepted being treated as an inferior being, to one hell of a tough woman that I am today. The benefits of being that tough woman who is not afraid to dare are so immense that I can't wait to share them with you and show you the exact principles that I followed to get to become a different person.

If you have the radical spirit in you, it means you are willing to try anything that can improve your life. At least take a glance, and your life will never remain the same. If you are a radical being, it also means you trust your instincts and you know I have some helpful things to share with you.

If you can think of one other person, you believe would benefit from this book, please share with them. Feel free to request for a free digital copy any time.

How to Use this Book

Pick up the principles in this book and internalise them. Apply them in your everyday life. They will help you to understand your journey and navigate the world better.

2

WHAT'S IN YOUR WAY?

What is your excuse? What are the roadblocks preventing you from living the life of your dreams? What pictures are you painting and what stories are you telling yourself? Some factors have been identified in this chapter to help you identify them too and rise above them.

The Slave Girl Complex

In today's society, most women like the slave girl are waiting for a Prince in shining armour to come to sweep them off their feet and take them to his castle to be his Princess. This is the nucleus of women's problems. It is rooted in learned helplessness. Women have this secret wish to be saved and taken care of by a man. They grow up to believe that "this is their reality". The media and society continue to teach them to embrace this position. Thus they believe that it's a man's place to take care of them. Some even voice it out. "... I need a man to take care of me". When at Prince Charming's castle, their problems will be entirely over - so they think.

Sometimes these dreams come true but what they fail to realise is that, when this happens, the prince has just bought himself another slave. In that house, you will have no voice or your own identity. But if he is a Prince and you are a Princess in your own rights - because you are relevant, you have something to contribute other than the mere fact that you are a woman and you are beautiful then you will relate with that Prince as an equal partner.

Or let's assume their dreams come true, but what happens if these women lose their husbands either to divorce or death? Or the man gets busy, or he is there but just disinterested?

Some other women aren't waiting for Prince Charming they are already married or on their own but in a relationship; they are laid back refusing to do anything – waiting for men to give them everything – including happiness. They do not work to better themselves or take responsibility for their happiness and choices. It breaks my heart when I see these women just acting helplessly and relying on men for basically all their needs – it's either their husband, boyfriend, father, uncle or a boss. So much so that, even when they pray they mention the name of this man who is their protector to provide ridiculously low needs. What stops them from being that person that will be mentioned in prayers by others and being an answer to other people's problems? They also crave attachment to this central figure in their lives, and they strive to be favourites.

Other sets of women that exist are those that have accepted mediocrity, so they do not make any effort to tap into their hidden potentials and contribute towards making the world a better place. Their excuse is, it's the job of the men to bring about development and these women (especially African women) to support their arguments, bring up religion and culture which places men in the dominant position.

The Slave Boy Complex

Some men are also culprits of the Slave Complex; just like women, they are looking for other people to transform their lives. They look at perceived successful people, and they think those people are supposed to take care of them because they have more. Just because maybe they are related, they work for this person or just knowing this person. They have different reasons they give for expecting, but bottom-line, there is a feeling of being entitled to some form of help and transformation from this person with perceived better circumstance. Another way to put it is "an entitlement mentality" sort of, you catch my drift now I guess.

The World owes us nothing. If anything is to be, it's up to us to create it. Whatever we receive we work for. Somehow someway it is paid for. If you receive without paying you will pay in the future. And when you refuse to pay favours forward, the flow will seize.

Why am I mentioning these sets of people?

It behoves you and me to identify them and educate them to become better. It's our business – all of us. You might say "it's not my business," "I want to mind my business;" Have you ever thought about how the world would be like if everyone said "it's not my business," "let me mind my business." Different technologies we use today that make life easier wouldn't exist. You wouldn't be reading this book as well.

We need to make it our business and strive to make a difference in the world. Make other people's lives better than what it is; find more straightforward ways, better ways of doing things. Educate people; make things more accessible and so on.

There are different ways in which you can serve, just identify which area suits you. But, **let's make it our business**.

You may not have to speak to anyone; just live right, and your life will serve as a model to a lot of people.

Standing Out in the World

To have a voice and stand out in the world, you won't go to sleep waiting for your dreams to come true or anchor on any successful person. You won't act like Cinderella and the slave girl - wait for the prince to fall in love with you, rescue you and take you to his castle then live happily ever after. If you think along these lines, it means you have neglected the fact that when a man whisks you to his castle, you too will become one of his acquired objects or a grand-maid in the castle. And like all other of his possession, you will have no say in how he runs his castle as well as his empire. For you to have a say, you have to be relevant to him and his kingdom, not one who is coming to be helped. Running to the castle for solace is running away from your life.

This principle applies to every gender, race, colour and social class across the world.

Relevance! Relevance! Relevance! Relevance!

Being relevant is the only answer. You can build your own empires and your castles too. When you are relevant in society, you will be needed. The World will know you, men and women will stick to you like bees. And when you have solutions to problems, the world will beat a path to your doorstep; it doesn't matter how you appear to people or the background you are from. Your results will announce you to the world. What you need to do is to work. First, show up and then start working. There are no shortcuts.

What then?

The questions you should always ask are: "how can I make an impact?" What service or product can I provide? What else can I do?

The answers to these questions and a little more will get you started on your journey and shape your life.

What We Owe Ourselves

The present realities call for a radical change that will instil the willingness to live beyond the limits of life. We need to be strong; not to compete with others, but for a higher expression of who we are.

3

WHO ARE YOU?

*I*t is highly essential to know who you are and your capabilities. The inner you is what is reflected in the outer you. It is how you see yourself, how you talk about yourself and how you act now in the present that is creating your life tomorrow. You need to know who you are, why you are here, and what you want from life.

What do you believe in and what do you stand for?

Everything you do will be guided by your definition of who you are and what you stand for. You need to be clear on what you believe in and what you stand for. This will inform your decisions and everything you do. It should be clearly reflected in everything you do.

Forget the way you were in the past. Discard past labels and start creating a new you. As a radical woman, it means you are deliberate, and you don't leave things to chance. Now is the time for you to start transforming your life into the life of your dreams.

Who is a Radical Woman?

Our radical woman is 'a doing woman'. "She's always doing something". "She is a very busy person". She wants to impact every life and everything thing she touches positively. She wants to make a great difference in the" World through her work. She is not wimpy or lethargic. She is tough but fair, and she says it as it is without any "garnishing."

What picture can you see in your mind of this tough but fair woman and all she is involved in? Powerful I guess.

The radical woman sets things in motion and creates her own plans; how she wants them and when she wants them. "She is not part of someone else's plans". "She has her own plans". If you don't have your own plans, you will become part of someone else's plans. Nigerians would say "She runs things, things don't run her".

She understands what she wants from life and goes for it with all she's got.

She is purpose driven, and she knows it. She is "a container with special contents sent to the universe on a mission for a purpose".

She does not accept bullying from people to get to where she wants nor does she let anyone dictate to her how to run her life. She is the architect as well as the director of her own life and she runs the show.

She is not afraid to shake the trees and see what falls. She also sets emotions aside in all her dealings. She learns how to get down in the mud without losing her dignity. She does all this with calm and confidence. This tells you the radical woman is developed in every sense of the word.

The radical woman is a diamond in the rough working towards a better version of herself every day. She acknowledges her mistakes and makes an effort to improve one step at a time, one day at a time. She overcomes challenges. Problems don't define her, they refine her.

If you are still reading this book, I believe you are a radical being already, or you are well on your way to becoming one as reading this is proof that you are in the transformation phase.

As a Radical Woman:
- You are travelling on this earth to find yourself.
- "You are not inferior to anyone". "You are a unique being". "You are a masterpiece". "You are one of a kind". "You are an authentic being not a poor copy of someone else".
- You have a vision.

- You foster healthy relationships, not relationships that deplete you.
- You are comfortable with who you are any day anytime.
- You are not looking for anyone to make you successful. You create how you want to be interpreted.
- You are intelligent. You are intuitive. You perceive things that are not visible to the naked eye.
- You are resilient.
- You are retrospective.
- You don't have to ask anyone what they think you tell them "don't think".
- You are a powerful being.
- You are an enterprising being. You create wealth.
- You are a rational being.
- You never compromise your integrity.
- You are an ethical being. You tell the truth and stand by the truth at all times.
- You stand out anywhere you are.
- You are cautious. You don't do things that will make you fall out of favour with the universe by trying to impress anyone or forge ahead.
- You have spiritual nostrils that help you to discern.
- You discern the forces dragging anybody to you.

Now

This is life, and there are no dress rehearsals. The show is on, and you are the heroine in it. What kind of a heroine do you want to be? What kind of traits do you admire in your movie and real life heroes and heroines?

Do you believe you can turn out like these heroes? Yes, you can! You only need to follow the same principles and laws that those real life heroes you admire follow and you too will be the perfect heroine of your own life that others will like to watch.

4

FUNDAMENTALS

Going through life not knowing what to do, being wimpy, lazy and sit around waiting for manna to fall on one's laps from heaven; even when it falls, which it does sometimes, not knowing what to do with it. Not taking initiatives or kick-starting anything; waiting for people to do things for one, blaming people, situations and things for sufferings and predicaments; not taking responsibility for actions and decisions… Do these lines sound familiar?

Transiting From Being Passive to Being Active

I must confess that at some point I was partly that person just described, but everything changed the day I woke up and realised that help was not coming from anywhere and no miracle was going to happen to transform my life to the way I want it if I did nothing. I realised no fairy godfather, nor godmother was going to wave a magic wand...to transport the life of my dreams to my feet.

I came to the realisation that my life was not going to change except I changed it. And help was not going to come from anywhere other than the "help" I gave myself. I woke up and smelled the coffee; from that day I got to work. I began to dream and have been working one day at a time to realise the life of my dreams. I also made the decision I wasn't going to put my destiny into anybody's hands anymore. I started working very hard to create my universe the way I wanted it to be. The outcome I got, nothing on earth can be compared, I must confess. I began to see the world through my own eyes and not through anyone's particular perspective. I got a renewed confidence in myself and in my abilities. I designed my life exactly how I wanted it, and I've been moving gradually towards it; fighting with direction and focus; giving to life what I want it to give back to me; not waiting to reap where I did not sow and above all, I am sowing continuously to reap a bountiful harvest.

The realisation also that nobody really cares about my problems and some are indeed happy that I even have them in the first place helps me to look within always for answers and to forge ahead without complaining. Instead of complaining I look for answers.

I am not where I want to be yet, but I am certainly not where I used to be either, and so far I've made tremendous progress and have been seeing amazing results daily. Every day I discover new potentials I never even knew I had. All these became possible the moment I went on from being passive to being active in my life's script.

You can't imagine the transformation I went through. Within a short time, I transformed to be a woman I love so much to perfection. Something exciting to note, if you see me now, you would think I was born this way. I hardly even remember being the opposite myself.

Yeah! Before this transformation, I appeared "strong" on the outside and was "strong" in some aspects, but not all and mistakes in my weak areas got me heartbroken sometimes they affected my entire being and made me vulnerable but following the principles and laws laid out in this book made me a radical woman and gave me completeness. When you are complete in yourself, you become an unstoppable force of nature and would dare to be anything you want to be. Your life can change too if you follow these same principles.

We have to understand that greatness is not being born with a silver spoon in your mouth. It is about following your dreams and realising the potentials that lie within you; and touching other lives with your gift. Thus, we need to make a firm decision to accept responsibility for our lives. When you choose to take charge of your life, then you know if anything is to be it's up to you to make it happen.

Before You Get Started

Understand that, the journey you are about to embark on is not an easy one. But you have to decide what you want for yourself, a better you who is capable of making an impact and leaving her footprints in the sands of time or same old boring you. The choice is yours.

You have to decide on what you want and be ready to pay the price no matter the cost. You must pay the price in full. You must sow before you reap and you may have to work long hours, days, weeks and years before you harvest the fruits of your investment.

Everything worthwhile takes time. Thus you need to invest long hours of hard work, discipline, dedication and persistence. Your work will delineate you from the crowd and put you in the class you want to be, sometimes above and beyond what you dreamed of.

You will have to move out of your comfort zone and risk feeling awkward and uncomfortable as you step into new frontiers. A shark will never outgrow its environment. Put it in a pond, and it will grow only a few feet, but put it in the ocean, and it will grow up to be as big as twenty feet long.

You must consciously and deliberately counter the pull of the comfort zone as you move upward and onward toward achieving the status of a radical woman who is on her way to bringing about transformations in the world.

Tradeoffs

The highly essential things in life usually take longer than we expect and cost more than we anticipate. You will need to determine what you will trade off for that dream. You will have to sacrifice something of value for that dream. Time, money, immediate gratification, etc. determine the price to pay to achieve your goal and then get busy paying that price.

When you have a goal, there are some things people will not know you like, because you are delaying gratification.

It's not very hard to give up little to grow when you have very little. The reason being, because your "everything" is not really much of "anything" at this point. But when you have started to earn some things, it becomes even more difficult. For instance, a great job you love, a beautiful environment, a cozy home, a particular image, some relationships and activities you enjoy. Would you give up these things to achieve your goals and live the life of your dreams?

You have to sacrifice uncommon things too for extraordinary dreams.

More Levels More Demons

Just as every opportunity provides at least one more "opportunity", so does each success gets you an admission ticket to more difficult challenges. This is the only path to growth. Thus, you need always to be prepared for them and make a firm commitment to learning always. Because the skills that got you here, more often than not will not get you to your next level. And to learn and grow you will keep sacrificing.

About Miracles

Yes, miracles happen! The moment you take responsibility and start working hard to achieve your dreams, the universe will conspire to help you. You will meet with different people, solutions, ideas, and so on that take you further in your pursuit. Most are chance encounters. The universe will bring them to you. Hence you must first develop a burning desire and take steps. Realise 'you first'. If you do nothing, you will receive nothing.

When you find the burning desire to be or do something, you have built a powerful force that can cut through any impossible circumstances and limitations.

Redefining You

Key Questions to Ask

- What do you really want to do with your life?
- What stories do you want to hear people telling about you?
- How do you want people to describe you?
- How can you achieve the life of your dreams?
- What would you need?
- Who would you need in the process?
- What expertise would you require?
- Where would you go?
- Why do you want this life?
- What kind of difference would you like to make in the world?
- What legacies do you want to leave behind?

These questions and a little more will guide you, and you will become outstanding in the years ahead. Look for the simplest most direct way to get from where you are to where you want to go, then get busy.

Next, take action. Remember, the best ideas in the world are valueless until they are implemented.

5

THE TRANSFORMATIVE PROCESS

It Starts From Within

Everything you are today is as a result of your thoughts up until now. You are not going to become successful until you look within. It is within not without. Your greatest journey on earth is not to visit Dubai, Australia, England, Africa or the United States, it is to find yourself. You will have to wrestle internally to find out who you are and what you are destined to do. You also wrestle with your mind to find out the right direction to follow. The good news though, is that "You will find answers." You will find the answers through people and strange situations you may never think of.

Everything you are or will ever be will be as a result of the way you think, thus if you change the quality of your thinking, you will change your life. You need to choose the thoughts that you dwell on. Rise above the distractions. You can't control anything or anyone in your life, but you can control your thoughts about them.

If your life is not going the direction that you want it to go, start thinking about where you want it to go. Good thoughts will produce good results just as negative thoughts will produce negative results; in essence, what you feed your mind with is the foundation of it all.

If you want to be a better person, you must change your thoughts now. You cannot change your yesterday, but you can do something about your today that can change your tomorrow. It doesn't matter the kind of circumstances in which you were born or what has happened or what you have gone through; that was yesterday. It doesn't matter what happened over the last five years, or during the previous ten years. That is your history not your divine purpose on earth; you may not be able to change all that, but, you can reposition yourself today. You have to make new decisions today that will change what your tomorrow will bring.

The way you define yourself that is the way you are; hence, you need to change your thoughts about yourself. Do not let anybody define you for you. As a matter of fact, you are indefinable as you are evolving every day. The person you will be tomorrow will be a version of who you are today. You are becoming a better you every day.

You need to activate positive thoughts; believe and invest in your future. Reject mediocrity and deliberately refuse to live your life on the sidelines. No matter your foundation, you can become a better you and possess all the good things of life. You may have been born poor, or have been brought up poor, but you are not here to be poor. You have the ultimate power to change the trajectory of your life, but first, the change starts with your thoughts.

The time to start is now. You have to take action. Build the thoughts and start acting every day one step at a time and you will change your future and get much more than you ever dreamed of.

You will only be poor if you think of yourself as "poor". You will only be invisible if you think of yourself as one. There is no way you will be making an impact in the world and remain unseen. You will become known, not as if you care, but it is a by-product of your actions and activities. You will also attract the best people in the word because you are one.

When you perform excellently, you will sit with elders at the adult table. You will sit among kings; princes and princesses will honour you. You cannot welcome in your thoughts whatever you don't want to permit in your life, because in a matter of time, what you have in your mind will come to life. Sweep the low mentality; sweep the conformity; be transformed in your mind and dare to be different.

Real change is someone who has changed her mind. Change her house, change her clothes; make her comfortable; there still will be no change until you change her mind. As a matter of fact, when someone has a slave mentality, there is nothing you can do for them. A slave is a slave. The fact that people have money doesn't mean they are prosperous in their mind. They could have money and still have a low mentality. Don't get caught in that; discard low life mentality.

You will excel to the degree of your thoughts and vision. To the degree of investment in your mind is what you exhibit. Focus! Be focused! Focus consumes you. The mind is the only weapon that can help you turn every mountain to a goldmine. Don't think like your cousins, friends, those you grew up with, people around you. Dare to be different and think differently.

You can lose everything but not your mind. It's a potent force; I can't stress it enough. If you see yourself now as you wish to be, and you walk, talk and behave like the very best person you can imagine yourself being, those dominant thoughts and goals will become your reality.

So Who Are You in Your Mind?

"You are who you think you are!"

Your self-concept and self-ideal will determine to a large extent how high you will climb in life. Your self-concept is how you see yourself. Your self-ideal is the person you wish to be. In essence, those two terms mean how you see yourself now and how you want to see yourself in the future. Your picture of these two personas will define the things you do and who you will become. This will also define your goals and everything you want for yourself.

What You Need on Your Transformation Journey

Only goals with careful planning and taking action will get you to your dream life. You cannot succeed without goals and a blueprint to achieve your goals; just like you cannot expect to win any game without a strategy and knowing the rules of the game. You have to "deliberately set goals and plan". You have to take full responsibility for your goals and get to work. All the principles you will learn in this book can only be applied while working. There's no room for manipulation whatsoever.

Dare to Dream an Uncommon Dream

You are as big as you imagined or conceived in your mind. No more no less. Hence dare to dream big! Dare to dream an exceptional dream! However, an exceptional dream requires exceptional effort and exceptional faith.

Everything is achievable if you can conceive it and believe it. Conceptualise it and get to work one day at a time; eventually, your dream will become a reality.

The seasons of your life will definitely change every time you dare to dream extraordinary dreams and start acting on them. Your belief in your dreams will determine if you will succeed or not. The clearer your dreams are, the higher your chances of success.

An exceptional dream may also take time to be realised and longer time to start bearing fruits, but when the fruits start coming, you will know it was worth every bit of the process.

Never underestimate yourself and sell yourself short. By underestimating yourself, you set either no goals or small goals that are far below what you are truly capable of accomplishing. Dream an extraordinary dream, believe it and get to work one day at a time, one step at a time towards achieving that height.

> *Far better it is to dare mighty things, to win glorious triumphs even though checkered by failures, than to run with those poor spirits who neither enjoy much nor suffer much because they live in the grey twilight that knows not victory nor defeat.*
>
> -Theodore Roosevelt

Dare to Be Different

Your relevance to yourself and to society is not in your similarity to others, but in your point of difference from others; hence you have to embrace your difference. That which makes you different is more important than your weakness. It's that special thing about you that is your calling. You don't have to be like any other person; you are unique just as you are. And, don't waste time dwelling on your weaknesses either, the rest of the world are already performing that for you.

Your calling moves you like nothing else in life. It fills you with joy and sets your heart on fire when you do it.

You will need to fight to be different. Life requires you to be a warrior to make a difference. To step out of the ordinary, you will have to compete strongly with the status quo. You can't be significant to yourself and the world by being ordinary; you work and fight for it. You will pass through hurdles to get there.

You've got to do your own growing up irrespective of how tall your grandmother was.

Ask Questions

Questions are about the most powerful things on earth. Life and business run on questions not on answers. Enough questions will make your decision making easy. Until you ask the right questions, you cannot find the right answers that you seek. Good questions produce great answers, and great answers produce great decisions; eventually great solutions.

Dare to ask questions. The unasked question is what keeps you at the disadvantage level. Changes in your life will take place at the heels of your questions.

Until you ask a question, others definitely control your information. You will only find answers to your questions when you ask them. Without questions even when you find answers you don't know if they could be answers.

6

DECISIONS

Every Radical Change is One Decision Away

Your transformation begins with a decision to be more than what you are today; a decision to experience more, a decision to experience a different feeling, a decision to be a success. The decisions lead you to set the required goals that will change your life radically.

Your decisions about what to channel your energies to, what things mean to you and what to do to create the results you desire in life control your destiny. The choices you make will lead you to ask questions on how to achieve those goals, and then you will decide what you need to do to get what it is you want.

Every decision you make will reveal your faith or your doubt. You may not be conscious of it, but it will be right there.

Whatever decision you take, that is what you will be.

Who you are right now is predicated on the decisions you have made up until now. But, news flash! Never allow who you are today and your present circumstances to sabotage who you are going to be tomorrow. Yesterday is your past, not your destiny. Your better days are ahead of you. You can start making good decisions right now that will change your life completely. God created us to be individuals that will prevail. We were born to maximise our potentials.

Every day you are going to have options for different opportunities. You are going to have choices to make decisions every day. "The choices you make will either make you or mar your future." "The decisions you make today will determine your tomorrow." Thus you have to be extremely careful.

Challenge yourself for the best future. Decide to be successful, happy, impactful, famous, powerful; and to have quality relationships. Decide to be relevant to yourself and to society at large. Decide to make a difference in the world. Decide to be a problem solver. Decide to see life through your own eyes and nobody else's. And decide to pay the price for whatever it is you want.

People who succeed are people who have built immunity to pain.

The Decision between Pain and Pleasure

Most of the decisions you make in life will revolve around "pain and pleasure". At every given time you are either deciding to evade pain or gain pleasure. The things you seek are either constantly tilting towards reducing pain or increasing pleasure. Reduce pain or gain pleasure? The feeling you desire is one decision away. This is always a tough decision you have to make every moment of every day of your life.

Pain sometimes can change our lives. We seem to need the push of frustration and distress before we open ourselves up to new ideas and ways of doing things. Reaching a level of pain we are not willing to settle for anymore, "when we are sick and tired of being sick and tired," we decide "no more;" this is the magical moment as described by Anthony Robbins "when pain becomes our best friend". At this point, we begin to ask how we can get out of this pain and never have to experience it again. The answers to these question and the actions we decide to take change our lives completely. If you scrutinise your life carefully, you will trace your growth to one form of pain or the other that turned everything around for you.

Pain could be associated with any of the following circumstances: poverty, failed relationships, rejection, low self-esteem, identity issues, loss of job, loss of a loved one, abuse, loss of business, loss of friendship, loss of respect from the people you love, and fear amongst others. Pain is pain no matter the circumstances. And extreme pain produces revolutionary ideas. Your decisions on how to handle these painful situations you have gone through are imperative to your success. At the end of the day, you will find that determining not to ever go through this kind of pain again made you grow more than you ever dreamed of. Pain is thus indeed "the touchstone for growth." Not sure who said this but I read it somewhere, and I wholeheartedly agree.

On the other hand, your decision to seek more pleasure, more peace of mind also changes your life. You are avoiding pain by seeking pleasure. You decide you want more of what you have; you want more to make your life more enjoyable. These steps you take to gain pleasure take you away from pain.

Very importantly, if you don't plan for pleasure, you will reap pain. You have to seek pleasure deliberately. Do not leave this great decision to chance.

Own Your Decisions

No one can force you to make decisions and take actions that run contrary to your values and aspirations. You are responsible for every decision. You created the life you are living today. You are not a victim of circumstances. The circumstances you are living in today are created by the decisions you made yesterday. Likewise, your future is entirely up to you. If you are feeling stuck, going in circles, this most probably is as a result of you being afraid to take the necessary risks to achieve your goals and live the life of your dreams.

Your decision to be a radical woman is entirely up to you. It is a decision only you have to make. It's up to you to decide to be free, powerful and to reach your highest potential without letting any situation, circumstance, person or anything hinder you.

When it is time to take action, remember that it's always better to be at the bottom of the ladder that you want to climb than at the top of the one you don't.

The best day of your life is the day you decide to be responsible for your choices.

Take Responsibility

You can dream big dreams, learn how to control both your conscious and subconscious mind and improve your self-concept and performance; but none of these efforts will give you any lasting results until you embrace personal responsibility.

You are responsible for your outcome in life!

Growing up is taking responsibility. When you become an adult, you take responsibility for your future. You need to make a firm decision that your life is your own without apologies or excuses; no one to lean on, rely on or blame.

The truth is, you cannot move from this level without taking full responsibility. There is a direct relationship between how much trust you are willing to accept and how high you will rise in life. The amount of responsibility you are willing to take will determine your income, your status, your level of prestige and the recognition you receive.

Become Responsible! Do what you have to do to achieve all you desire in life. Many people cry for help, and because there are no answers to their call for help, they feel the pangs and pains of neglect. Don't be like these people. When you realise you own your life and it's up to you to make it an amazing journey, your life begins to unfold from this moment of awakening.

In the words of Albert F. Geoffrey, when you take charge of your life, there is no longer need to ask permission of other people or society at large. When you ask permission, you give that person power over your life. Quit blaming anybody for your situation. You are absolutely responsible for everything you are today and what you will become tomorrow. You are accountable for everything you say or do and for even what you don't say or don't do. Refuse to make excuses or to blame others; instead, make progress towards your goals. You can and will do better.

Decide to Love and Believe in Yourself

Life is not the way it is supposed to be, it's the way it is. "The way you cope with it is what makes the difference" observes Virginia Satir. I couldn't agree any less. Life is what it is. Your job is to make your life a masterpiece. Deliberately and systematically create the circumstances that raise your-self-esteem in everything you do. Live your life as if you were already the outstanding person you intend to be sometime in the future. While we don't always get what we want, we always get what we choose.

You have to believe in yourself for you will never get anybody to believe in you until you believe in yourself. You have to, first of all, believe in yourself.

You will never get anybody to help you until you help yourself. You will never get anybody to love you until you love yourself. If you don't love yourself no one else will. Your belief and passion will carry you through every difficult situation or any challenging circumstances, and enable you to realise your dreams ultimately.

People want to associate with what is cherished. People will love you to the amount of love you have for yourself. Make a conscious decision to continuously engage in activities and do things that make you love yourself more and more every day.

Ensure everything you do is consistent with increasing the amount of love and respect you have for yourself and that others have for you. Ask yourself: "What kind of a person do I have to be to live the kind of life I want to live and to earn the respect of the people I care about?" Who are those people whose love and respect are important to you? What do you have to do and who do you have to become for them to love and respect you?

Remind yourself that you have exceptionally powerful abilities and that you will know exactly how to use them when the occasion calls.

The secret to loving yourself more is to be consistently setting goals and keep taking actions one step at a time. The decision to become a goal-setting, goal achieving, future-focused person gives you a tremendous sense of control. You feel wonderful about yourself. You feel that you are the master of your own destiny.

Your self-esteem increases as you progress toward your goals. You like and respect yourself more and more. Your personality improves, and you become a more positive, confident person. You feel happy and excited about life. You open the floodgates of your potentials and begin moving faster and faster toward becoming all that you were meant to be. At this level, you begin to attract other successful people like yourself. You also start dropping people that waste your time or try to drain you because you see clearly now.

I can't say it enough; if you don't believe in yourself, no one else will. No one is willing to bet on you if you have never done anything before. People need to see convincing results. At the right time, you will understand.

Believe in your dream and believe in you, the heroine within you doesn't just believe you can achieve your goals, it knows you will realise them. People will trust you when you trust yourself. Confidence is all we need on this journey, but confidence doesn't come from what others think of you. It comes from within. When you believe in yourself, you can do anything you want. All you need is practice. No one was born skilled in any field or quality, they learned. You can lean too and become good at anything you want. So, roll up your sleeves and find a way to live that dream you have.

Again, Decide to Embrace Your Difference

As earlier iterated, accept who you are and embrace what makes you different instead of trying to change who you are. Your relevance is not in your similarity to other people but in your point of difference from others. Your difference from others is what makes you unique. That is what sets you apart and holds the key to your divine purpose on earth. We all have the potential. Your potential is attached to your purpose in life, and your purpose is connected to your success. If you don't know what you are here to do, you can't succeed.

It pays to be different. Celebrate it. It's your difference that is monetising. Everything in life is bought. You trade your difference. Even in relationships, you buy with integrity, honour and so on. Everything is bought just the currency changes.

More often than not, your weaknesses are blessings in disguise. Some successful women attest that, if they had been extremely beautiful, tall, charismatic, gorgeous, comfortable and extra intelligent they would have never had become so productive. This is because they would never have had the need to work so hard to develop themselves. Acceptance makes you relax but when you don't fit in perfectly, or you are rejected you work extra hard to excel.

7

SETTING YOUR GOALS

A goal is something you are trying to do or achieve. It is the desired result that a person or a system envisions, plans and commit to achieving. Those who have goals achieve more than those who do not have. Even if you did not reach them, your life would be better than where you started.

Goal setting is when you begin to attach measurable time and structures to achieve your desires. When you have goals, you will have a purposeful existence. You will be focused, and you will be different from your contemporaries.

You cannot live by default; you have to set goals always. Goals are the fuel in the fire of achievement. A person without goals is like a traveller moving aimlessly without direction. Your goals give you purposeful existence. Decide exactly what it is you want and go after it. Determine to pay the price in full and in advance.

You sow goals, and you reap results. People who do not have goals have no choice but to work for those who do. It's either you are working to achieve your own goals, or you are working work to fulfil someone else's goals. Look within you and see what you can do. Your acres of diamonds probably lie right under your own feet. They are more often than not disguised in some form of "not so brilliant sight".

Great things won't stroll to you; you will need to seize them. You are going to have to be deliberate in setting goals and working to realise those goals. Take action! "The only action is action, and nothing else counts much. A million brilliant ideas without action are pointless. Don't tell people what you are going to do, show them.

The rewards of setting goals are innumerable. Your goals will set you apart in society. Your goals will place the spotlight on you. Goals will distinguish you. Yes! Absolutely!

Everyone that has received anything worthwhile worked for it. Once you understand you need to work for what you want, living becomes a different ball game. Everything you do will be with deliberate intention. Your goals will determine what you say no to and what you say yes to in every situation.

Define Your Goals and Focus On the Ultimate Result

Visualise every step to the end. If you can conceive it, you can make it happen. When you focus on your goals, you regain a sense of control over your life; your self-esteem rises, so does your self-confidence; you sense that what happens around you doesn't have to affect what is within you.

At every time you have to find a direction for your life. This direction is reflected in the walk towards your goals. It will direct you. If you don't decide where you are going, life will take you to a place you probably never wanted to be. You may not be able to put a stop to unexpected occurrences in your life, but you can choose to take positive steps that make the most of them.

You have the ultimate power to set goals and to go after them. Without goals, you are a lost cause. No matter the circumstances you find yourself, you must set goals and chase them with all your might. So many people have overcome tremendous challenges and succeeded in life. You too can do it.

Setting goals, working toward them every day and finally achieving them is the key to happiness. Goals are so powerful that the very act of thinking about them makes you happy, even before you start working to achieve them. Thus, you have to set goals for every day of your life. Even when you want to spend the day in bed, let it be part of the plan. Don't leave things to chance; be deliberate in everything.

Test Your Goals

The starting point of setting and achieving goals is projecting forward and asking yourself, "If everything happens perfectly, what will my future look like?" Every person who became truly successful could see into the future well in advance of it becoming a reality.

As you project into the future, your goals must be:
- Specific. Specify clearly what it is you want. Your vision needs to be clear for you to succeed.
- Measurable: Fix time to make it happen and continuously measure your progress as you go.
- Time-sensitive. Work with a timeline and also develop a long-term perspective. When you visualise your ideal life in a year, five years, and ten years from now, the next step is always to ask yourself what actions you need to take in the present.
- Personalised. Personalise your goals. You are responsible.
- Realistic. Must be something realisable and significant.
- Attainable. Don't take on too much by trying to appear more significant than you are. Make your goals achievable.
- Written down. Write down the vision. Say it Write it in the present tense as if it has already happened.
- Exciting. They must excite you. You must be passionate about your goal.

Believe in your strategy and get to work. You will meet detours now and then, but they are all part of the plan. Every challenge you meet will make you a better person.

Focus and Clarity

Clear goals enable you to unleash your full potential for personal and professional success. When you set big, exciting goals for yourself and the person you want to be, and then think about these things every day, you take full control of the direction of your life.

Clear, exciting goals and ideas help you to act deliberately with focus: the clearer your goals, the higher your chances of success. You will begin to feel happier about yourself and your entire world, and you will become more positive, optimistic, cheerful and enthusiastic. You will begin to feel motivated from within to get up and get going every morning because every step you take is moving you a step closer to something important.

The clearer you can be about your long term future, the more rapidly you will attract people and circumstances into your life to assist in making that future a reality.

The more clarity you have about who you are and what you want in life, the more you will attain, and the faster and easier you will achieve it in every area of your life.

You have to remove distractions. Guard the doorways of your mind diligently and remain focused on what is important to you. Dwell on your desires for the future and refuse to entertain fears and doubts. Focus your mind on what can be done in the future rather than what has happened in the past. By staying focussed, you will accomplish extraordinary things in the same amount of time that the average person spends just living day to day.

Structure and Orderliness

The secret of your success is within your daily routine. Organise your day, week or year according to your purpose and priorities; this will give you clarity of thought and strengthen everything you do.

When you know your purpose and priorities, and you become well organised as well, you feel a sense of power. You will be acting with a goal every minute of every hour of every day. You will respect yourself more, and people will get to recognise you too.

You must, therefore, pay close attention to how you spend every minute of every hour of every day. Sow into every day.

You Must Plan

The first key to planning is visualising the process of what it will take to achieve your goals. It's like a mental rehearsal, projecting in your mind pictures of yourself doing, acting and succeeding in your course. Your visual images become your reality. They intensify your desires and deepen your beliefs. They increase your willpower and build your persistence.

Make plans and each day spend your time achieving these goals.

It's necessary for you to have short-term goals and long term goals. I mean, it's best if you had goals for today, goals for five, ten and twenty years from today.

The ideal short-term goal for business, career and personal planning is about ninety days. The ideal long-term period for the same goals is two to three years. These time frames seem to be the model time for continuous motivation.

When you set a significant goal for two three and five years, you can then break it down to ninety-day segments, and subsequently break those down to monthly, weekly and daily sub-goals with measurable benchmarks to enable you to assess your progress.

Write out in detail what you want, when you want it, why you want it and where you are starting. Make a list of all you need to achieve your goal, the obstacles you must overcome, the information you will need and the people whose help you will need.

The more detailed your plans and the better organised your ideas, the more likely you are to achieve your goals on schedule and precisely as you defined them. A good list gives you a track to run on and dramatically increases the likelihood of your achieving your goal. The plan may keep getting adjusted time and time again, but eventually, you will have a rock solid plan that will work for you.

Now that you have a plan to take action, take action now. Try your possible best to do something every day that will move you toward the achievement of your primary goals. You must develop the success habit by doing something every day to move you toward your goals. Review them every day and always be looking for something you can do to contribute to their realisation. The most brilliant plan in the world without action is useless.

Start One Day at a Time

The journey of a thousand miles starts with a step. Take one step at a time; one day at a time; provided you don't stop. Decide to keep moving no matter what. Whether it's by flying, walking or crawling, it doesn't matter. The most important thing is that you are moving forward. If you continue moving forward, definitely you will get to your set destination. Some days you are not going to feel like it, in fact, most days you are not going to feel like it, but you have to find a way to keep yourself inspired and keep moving. Never be on one spot. No matter how slow you go, don't stop. Keep moving. After many years you will be amazed how far you have come.

For me those moments and days I don't feel like it, I launch into action when it is time for that task. I find that in less than ten minutes into that task I get motivated and begin to perform outstandingly. It has always worked for me so all I try to do is get to work anyway and I conquer inertia.

Face tasks and challenges one step at a time, one day at a time; this is a great way to stop worrying. Take on challenges, issues or problems inch by inch. Don't try to complete everything at ones. No matter how difficult a task or challenge is, doing something about it gradually, one day at a time, you will see its completion or accomplishment.

While doing my PhD program, the process looked so long and looking at all I had to do, was enough to overwhelm me. Then I started practising writing a few hours every day. Sometimes it would take a month or more to finish a chapter or corrections from my supervisors, but in 2017 I completed the program. I learnt a valuable lesson from the process; "any task you keep tackling little by little daily will be completed". More often than not, the moment you get to work you overcome inertia, and you start working with unimaginable speed.

8

ON YOUR JOURNEY

Staying Inspired

The ability to keep yourself inspired is one of the most significant skills you will ever learn in life. When you are inspired there is nothing you cannot do. Find the stream of inspiration and live there.
If you find yourself with a lackadaisical attitude, down, unmotivated, and unwilling to take action, remind yourself you can't let down you're a- Team - the people who believe in you and have worked on you in the past.

My parents and siblings believe I am an unstoppable force of nature. They think I am capable of a lot. So, when things get tough, and I am tempted to give up, I remember them and determined not to let myself or them down, I keep pushing.

It's not always easy to stay motivated at difficult times, but finding that proper balance will eventually come naturally to you such that whenever your positive attitude seems threatened, you will be able to centre yourself mentally, focus on your long term goals and avoid being knocked off course by circumstances, feelings or anyone. It is helpful in difficult times to call up the positive and supportive people who motivate you. These people believe in you and your ability to succeed.

No matter what happens to me, chatting with my twin sister for only a few minutes, I get back on track stronger than before.

Also exercising, relaxing, going on vacation and other activities help me to unwind and come back refreshed.

Discipline

We need discipline. On your journey, motivation will get you going, but discipline keeps you growing. No matter how talented you are or how many opportunities you receive, if you want to excel, you must make discipline a part of you.

Discipline puts pressure on you to realise your potential. Even in your mind constructions or visualisations, you need discipline. When you think about something, the object or subject gets drawn towards you. You have to hold the thought long enough for it to come to you. No distractions.

Discipline your energy to express it in a useful way. Once you have the energy, you have to convert it into something useful to you and society at large.

You are a wealth creator; thus you need the energy to create wealth. Use your energy to create wealth and to make an impact in the world. Discipline yourself to convert your energy towards a definite cause.

Discipline and force yourself into a particular profession. Don't be over the place. If you say no to the wrong things, you will be able to say yes to the right things.

We need discipline to guard our reputation. Your reputation is your life; guard it with your life. Don't let your private life destroy your public life of success. You have to discipline yourself to be useful to yourself and society.

Time Management

The difference between successful people and losers is how they manage their time. Successful people manage their time effectively and efficiently. Without proper management of your time, you cannot succeed. You need to discipline yourself in managing your resources and time to achieve success.

Your respect for time is a prediction of your future. Life is not a game where you have extra time; this is life, there are no rehearsals, and the show is on. Each of us goes on stage cold with no prior knowledge or preparation. We have to act any which way. We fail, we make mistakes, but the show is on. What are you going to do about this scene and your next scene?

You need to be clear about your goals and manage your time properly. I have never seen any successful man or woman who does not value his or her time. Losers and poor people have no value for their time; they spend it on mundane things and 'go nowheres' like them. They don't understand the precious nature of time.

You don't have extra time; therefore make everyday count. Save time! Keep track of your time. Invest your hours; do not spend them. Improve yourself every day! Introduce something new into your life every day that counts.

Time is transient. Tick Tock! When it goes, you never get it back. So we need to give it our best at every given time. It's in your interest to plan your time efficiently and effectively. Your level of success tomorrow will be to the degree of what you do with your time today. Just as your life today is a result of what you did with your time yesterday.

If you are busy chasing your goals, you won't have time to waste on people. Some people seem so busy running from one meeting to another meeting; others staying busy with mundane things; this is not the kind of being busy I'm talking about here. Success doesn't come from movement and activity. It comes from focus and ensuring your time is spent efficiently and productively. Therefore you need to be productively busy and engage in only those things that yield results.

You get the same number of hours in the day as everyone else, use yours wisely. Hang around only busy people, because they know the value of time. Time is money. Invest your time with people. When you are busy working, you have no time to be distracted; no time for anyone to make decisions for you. It then means you will have no time to spend on people. Your time is valuable to you. If you hang with people doing nothing you reap nothing. Nothing to nothing equals to nothing. Those who waste your time are your enemies. Make every moment count.

Every day is pregnant with opportunities. You have 86400 opportunities to do anything. Waste no second from this moment to the end of your life. You are the product of your output not of your effort, so use your time efficiently and effectively. Whatever you have been called to do on this earth; start doing it right now. The wait is over.

Don't spend so much time watching television. Time is of the essence. Get busy so that you too can be watched by others.

Advancing confidently in the direction of your dreams means doing what is important every day. Engaging in unproductive things does nothing for you. It merely uses up your time. Daily growth leads to personal advancement.

Always ask yourself, what is the most valuable use of my time right now? Is this the best use of my time?

Also, do not waste your time on what somebody else can do for you. Pay people to do things for you and focus on those things that only you can do well.

You only have so much time, anytime you decide to take on a new project or activity, determine what activity you are willing to drop for the new. You will have to determine where you are going to cut out time from for the new activity or project.

Determine Never to Be Idle

The only way to move toward a goal – no matter how big or small – is to take action. Positive thinking is essential but if left undirected and controlled can turn out to be positive wishing and "positive hoping". People who accomplish great deeds in life are intensely action-oriented. They are moving all the time. They are always busy, they have an idea, and they take action on it immediately. They are always in motion like moving targets. Low achievers and, on the other hand, are full of good intentions, but they always have an excuse for not taking action today.

Plan your life in such a way that you are busy all day round, all year round and the rest of your life. Get up and keep going all day.

Once you start going, keep going; don't stop. It's incredible how much we can get done when we are always doing something productive. Even when you are sleeping make sure it is part of the plan. When you are extremely busy, distractions get reduced.

Be productively busy always; this is where your real power lies. Productive activities give you ***personality weight.***

Develop a Sense of Urgency

Deliberately develop a sense of urgency and a pro-strategic mindset. Be proactive. Get to work as quickly as you can and try to finish as quickly as possible and move to the next thing. Also, increase your moving pace. The faster you move, the more energy you have, the happier you will be and the more enthusiastic and creative you will become. It is learnable. When you start acting with urgency, in no time at all, you will begin to work faster and smarter and feel successful. Laziness will begin to irritate you. Now don't waste this new gift; select your most important tasks then approach them with a sense of urgency. In no time at all, you will begin to feel this energy within you looking for more and more to accomplish. An unstoppable force that's what you will become. You can't fake it, it just comes.

Make Perseverance Your Middle Name

Great works are performed not by strength but by perseverance. Your determination to go on against all the odds is the key to success. Everything worthwhile takes time as earlier iterated. You must be willing to persevere for a long time without much evidence of progress. What you are aiming for is a fundamental long-term improvement in your life. It's taken you many years to become the person you are. You must be willing to work very hard to become someone different.

Expect the troubles, the odds, the crises but stand tall and look them in the eye when they come. Let them know you will defeat them. With this attitude, you will no longer be scared of challenges because they can't stop you, you will persevere no matter what; and, a whole new set of possibilities will open up to you.

Your willingness to persevere is the real measure of your belief in yourself and your ability to succeed. Each time you persevere against the odds, you build pride, power, self-esteem that will remain within you. You become stronger and more resolute. Every great person you see has had to endure and persevere through challenges before achieving astounding success. Their ability to endure and persist is the reason they are great; this is the only thing that guarantees that you will eventually be great. Make your mistakes but keep moving, don't quit.

Manage Disappointments with a Positive Attitude

No matter how experienced, careful or how well you organise yourself and everything you do, you will experience countless disappointments, setbacks, obstacles, betrayals and adversities. The higher and more challenging your goals are, the more disappointments and difficulties that will come to you.

However, it is impossible for us to grow and develop to our maximum potential unless we face adversities and learn from them. Life's greatest lessons come as a result of setbacks and temporary disappointments which we have done our utmost best to avoid. Disappointments are thus blessings to us in disguise.

Determine to See the Good in Perceived Adversity

The very best qualities of strength, courage, character and persistence are brought out in you when you face your most significant challenges, and you respond to them positively and constructively. What makes the difference between the ace and the low achievers is basically how the ace use adversity and struggles for growth while the others allow difficulties and challenges to crush them and leave them discouraged and dejected.

Set Deadlines

Set benchmarks and create scorecards, measures and deadlines for every task that you must complete on the way to any of your goals. Taking these steps will motivate and drive you at an unconscious level to start earlier, work harder, stay later and give your best shot.

The more you set and work towards deadlines, the more accurate you will become in predicting the time necessary to complete them.

Live in the Moment

You can't reach your full potential until you learn to live in the moment. No amount of guilt can change your past; likewise, no amount of apprehension can change the future. Embrace the reality of where you are at and decide to be happy no matter what.

Accept your past. Make peace with your past and move on to your future. Only look back to your history only once in a while to take some lessons there that you will apply in your future, not to look at to get sad.

Similarly, accept the uncertainty of the future. Worry has no place in the here and now. Most of the things we worry about never happen. It's best to cross the bridge when you get there never before it.

9

SOME FRUITS OF YOUR EFFORTS

Success

The successful life is actually a combination of successful days. It is made up of various ingredients, which include the physical, mental, emotional and spiritual. Each person needs a particular combination of these ingredients to feel the very best about herself and life.

When you have challenging goals you are moving towards without distractions, the world will give way for you, and you will become an unstoppable force. Naturally, without you trying, you will attract more and more people to you and eventually grow your influence. As you go on to become a successful person yourself, naturally, you will be relating with other successful people, because you will have dealings with them. You are relevant to them, and they are relevant to you. You don't achieve this by trying to impress them. ***A radical woman does not have to impress anyone just for "impressing" sake. She can be charming but she doesn't need the approval of anyone, she does what she wants to do, when and how. Success and Wealth come as a result of her seeds.***

It is a daily experience, and only you can decide what real success is to you. The key is not seeing how much you have acquired, or you can do but doing what you love doing with excellence, how you want it, when and where.

The greatest reward of success is not winning, the money you make, the wealth you acquire nor the promotion you receive, but rather the excellent person you become in the process of striving toward success and exerting self-discipline every time it is required.

Winning also is not nearly as important as being in the race. Being in the race is what qualifies you to pass through the process of refinement. Whether you come first position or not, it doesn't matter. What matters is, your going through the process. So at every point in time, you have to strive to enjoy the process. Be grateful for the process and enjoy it.

What Does Success Mean To You?

Define what success means to you. Start with a positive and fresh mindset, and compile a list.

"It doesn't matter where you're coming from; all that really matters is where you're going. And, where you're going is only limited by your imagination."

Your gender, family, colour of skin, country, age, and so on should not limit you. God decided them for you. You had no say. So they should never be limitations to you in any way.

Success without an understanding of the purpose is meaningless. Find out what God has brought you to do on earth at this time, in this age. Find the purpose and get busy working to achieve it. If you search within you, you will definitely find it. Having the intention will lead you right to it.

Power

"True power" is standing on a corner of the street waiting for no one in particular. Success, on the other hand, is the freedom to do what you want, when you want it and how you want it. This freedom gives you power over your life and everything as well as everyone in it. It gives you the highest state of happiness.

Redefining You

True Power and True Security

True power is being able to do things for yourself without having to rely on anyone. Being able to initiate change and get change.

Again, true power is "standing on the street waiting for no one in particular". Your job is to keep working every day on how to be self-reliant and have as many options available to you in everything you do.

Real power is being secure. It is giving yourself the security that you deserve. Any other security not from you is artificial. It can be taken away from you at any time, and you will become vulnerable and powerless once more. Basing your security on your job, how much money you earn from your job, how much money you have in the bank, the house you live in, the environment you live in, the people you know are all artificial sources. Your security should come from within you. Not from external sources. You can "want" things from people but not "need" but not get desperate such that you can't live without those things. When you don't get desperate and always seek options, nothing whatsoever can control you. Because when you can't have A, you look for B, when B is not possible you opt for C. You are at this point, on the driver's seat of your life. At this level, you experience extreme power over your life and everything around you. People will respect you, and you become like a magnet that everyone wants to be around. The simple secret is, "with or without anybody or anything in particular 'you are who you are". Nothing or nobody is a big deal.

It still all boils down to your goals. Staying true to your goals means you will have in abundance all you need because you are working towards abundance every day. It would suggest that you know how to make yourself happy, as you are not waiting for anyone to make you happy. Thus you are extremely busy with your journey.

It is only when you are busy with your goals that you will have little or no time for "go-nowheres". If you are sincerely moving towards your goals, you will have little or no time for any form of frivolities. You will choose to do only the important stuff because you don't have enough time. You will thus be scarce and valuable.

Have no time to worry about what other people think or say about you. Have no time to be distracted. You are more powerful than you think. Just focus on being the best that you can be and helping as many people that you can help in your time here.

Attaining this status isn't that easy, but it's easy as well if you follow the principles and steps. It starts with accepting responsibility for your life. Accept you are responsible for everything in your life – good or bad. Moreover, anything you desire; it's up to you to make it come to pass. "If it is to be it's up to you, no one else". After accepting responsibility, determine what it is you want to achieve in life. What is that unique thing you would do if you had no fear, doubts or limitations? How would you want to be remembered when you are no more? How much money do you want to earn? What profession do you want to pursue? What are the legacies you want to leave behind? Now, determine those things; write them out and get to work on those goals. Write out your plan and start immediately.

Eliminate powerlessness by taking action now. No work equals to irrelevance, dependency, no money, helplessness, no status and finally, equals to powerlessness.

Powerlessness breeds negative emotions and negative emotions breed evil thoughts. When you can't control your thoughts anymore, you start sinking.

Wealth

Wealth is not just about how much money you have. You are wealthy when you have in abundance something you love. It could be anything – health, finances, experiences, knowledge amongst others. Regarding financial wealth, the universe has given you the potential to create wealth. You are incredibly gifted and talented.

Don't wait till you have millions before you start creating wealth; begin from where you are. Your ideas will create wealth for you. You will receive rewards from the problems you solve for people. When you solve "unique problems", you will receive "unique rewards" and extraordinary financial wealth. Thus, your wealth will emanate from the problems you choose to solve for people.

Sowing and reaping

You reap what you sow. You are earning today precisely what you have decided to earn, no more and no less. If you are not happy with your current income, choose to earn more. Set it as a goal, make a plan, and get busy doing what you need to do to achieve what you want to earn.

If you want more, you will have to sow more. Every extra wealth comes from "extra sowing". It is required to put in a little extra each time, in your job, in your business and relationships. Add more value than you are paid for in all your transactions– be it in products or services.

It is your responsibility to determine the skills, competencies, abilities and resources you will need to make the kind of money you want to earn going forward. Find ways to make yourself more valuable in your world every day. All wealth comes from adding value, from producing more, better, cheaper, faster, easier, more accessible, more comfortable than others and much more than you did yesterday.

One good idea can save you years of hard work or much money. A compound of good ideas matched with the right action will make you wealthy, happy and successful.

Nevertheless, to accumulate wealth, you will need to take financial risks, work hard, be disciplined and focused. The harder you work, the luckier you become. More often than not, wealth is the result of hard work, perseverance and most of all self-discipline.

Take responsibility and trust in your abilities. Never rely on others wealth to make you wealthy. Appearances of wealth can be deceptive.

As you advance in your journey, you will realise that your greatest asset is not what you have stored in your bank accounts or your possessions, rather your earning ability. You should be able to multiply what you have. More so, if you lose it all, you are capable of making it all back even within a shorter time than it took you before.

If you are in the business of selling, realise that customers are 'collected one by one'. Be close to them; have empathy for their needs. Take time and energy to study what they need and make sure that you stock what reflects these needs.

Embracing the Law of Overcompensation

Cultivate the habit of always giving more than what you receive. Successful people and successful businesses are those that consistently exceed expectations, who continually do more than is expected of them.

If you want to increase the quantity and quality of your returns as well as your rewards, then you need to increase the quantity and quality of your service. By always doing more than you are paid for, you will eventually reap more than you are getting now. By putting more in, you will get more out. By over-contributing, you will end up being over-compensated.

Clarifying Some Myths about Wealth

Some people see wealth and the pursuit of wealth as evil, but wealth is not merely a means of personal enrichment. Wealth is a weapon that can be used to make the world a better place.

The selfish pursuit of money is an empty goal, but the search for the best that money can create is one of humanity's most significant responsibilities in our time here.

The more money you own, the more ability you have to change the lives of those who are in need positively. If you are someone poor and of good heart, you are not able to help much when people are in need. When they are in need that requires financial assistance, you will remain a good person but cannot help them with what they need the most. Given the same circumstances but you are wealthy; you can give to these people because you have resources in abundance for yourself and anyone around you who needs.

Financially disadvantaged people can do little to help others in the same situation, but the rich can support as many as they are able. If a person is rich, she has the opportunity to do good to people she encounters, but if this person is poor, she is unable to help anyone but herself. A poor person can save a life, but a wealthy person can build a hospital and save millions. The wealthy person can also build schools where others will receive education and in turn, become successful and help make the world a better place to live in for this generation and other generations to come.

In essence, those with the greatest wealth can do the greatest good for the most significant number of those below them. This is not to say the poor cannot help. Those with little can still do a lot. As in place of money, they can give positive actions that are of equal value to any charitable donations. Time and efforts are equally useful in helping to advance humanity.

It's therefore up to you, would you seek wealth to be able to help more people or do you want to be just comfortable for yourself alone?

Fame

Fame is a consequence of success. Whether you want it or not it will come to you when you are successful. Keep being busy and let your works announce you. Be famous for the things you do - the products you sell or the services you render. It is a more enduring way to be known.

Have something to give to the world, and you will be known all over the world. Your name will be on every lip. If you stumble upon fame without anything valuable to give, you will lose it within a short time. The truly successful people don't really care because they are so busy creating and solving. Be like these people. Have something for the world and the world will look for you. It doesn't matter whether you are black, white, red or green.

You owe yourself the duty of remaining relevant and making a difference in the world. You aim to impact and not to impress. A self-made confident person is not a person who is trying to impress anyone. You don't need people's approval to progress. Pay no attention to the accolades of others. Keep walking on your personally crafted tracks.

Happiness

You are happy to the degree of your being in control of your life. When you are in control of your life, you are happiest. However, happiness is different things to different people. Your definition of happiness may not be another person's definition.

Things that excite you may not make the other person happy. For me, I am happiest when I am productively busy. Inactivity gives me depression. At every point in my life, I set out different goals that keep me extremely busy. I am so busy that so many things don't bother me. I also do not have time for a lot of frivolities. I am happy whether I have children or not. I am at bliss whether I have a husband or not. I am in a state of perfect happiness whether I have a boyfriend or not. I find contentment in the way I am. I involve myself in many things that I care about so much so that I really do not have time to ponder about what you think of me or what you do not think. My concern is what I think of you. **My focus is on making everyone and everything I come in contact with every day better than I met them.** I am committed to touching lives even in the most subtle way. It gives me fulfillment and makes me happy. Challenges come from left and right, but I do not let them disturb my peace of mind. Once I am at peace, I am in an excellent state of bliss. So, I guard my inner peace.

I try my very best not to allow any negativity to get to my place of inner peace. However, what has helped me most is staying busy. I have worthy goals I am committed to every day that most of the troubles of this life don't get to me. Besides, I see every challenge or failure as a learning experience. The bigger the problem, the greater the lesson that will be learnt and the greater your character will be refined. So, I choose to see the good in everything.

In every situation that you encounter just like everyone that you have dealings with, they will either be a blessing or a lesson. No more no less. It's left for you to decide which one it is. When you live life with that attitude, nothing or no one really bothers you. Given any situation, if you have done all you could and still cannot handle the situation, walk away and keep your peace.

Do not give anyone the responsibility to make you happy. It's your sole responsibility. Someone might make you happy today but unable to tomorrow. Depending on anyone to make you happy is giving too much power to that person.

Nothing is worth your peace of mind. Not money, a job, a relationship, short term pleasures,…name it. Nothing whatsoever is worth it. I can't say it enough. Once your peace of mind is attacked, you can't be happy. You need your inner peace to be happy. No matter how fanciful that job, how handsome that man if it is not making you happy, ask yourself, is this worth my peace of mind? If your answer is no, move on. Determine what it costs you to keep some things in your life and ask yourself if it is worth it. Now, that doesn't mean quitting will give you the peace and happiness that you desire, you will have different challenges, different decisions to make and newer obstacles but you check if you can go through this one and still keep your inner peace.

If your actions are moving you gradually towards your desired goal, you will be able to bear many things as you see them as part of the price you have to pay for your desired goal.

Thus, once you have a goal, and you are moving gradually towards this goal every minute of every hour of every day, it means you are in control of your life. You do not let people or situations control you, because, at every moment, you are considering if what you are about to do or not do is leading you towards your goal. You are at this point in a position of power, and this gives you great happiness.

In every moment of every hour of every day, ask yourself if what you are doing or not doing is leading you towards your goal. How is this helping me or helping my audience? How is this conversation helping me or my audience? How is this action or inaction helping or not helping? When you find the answer, you do the right thing.

Yes, a new job, a new apartment, new clothes, new stuff can give you happiness, but here we are talking about lasting happiness that you feel every day whether things are good or things are bad. If you achieve all kind of stuff in the material world, but you lose your health or peace of mind, you get little or no pleasure from your other accomplishments.

Happiness Comes from Within

Money is necessary, it attracts more wealth and poverty might bring unhappiness, but money won't necessarily give you happiness. You could be living in that beautiful castle, driving the most expensive car in the world, dressing in the most expensive clothes and still be sad and depressed. Material things are not guarantees you will be happy. As you grow within you reach a new level of peace and profound happiness.

Reaching this level when you are in control of your life, you are not afraid to lose anything because you know how you got there in the first place and you know how to get it all over again. Yes, you will feel down some moments, days but you always get back up because you know what matters. Your goal is so important that you can't afford to slip away into depression or stop moving towards it. When you conclude one goal, start another, and another and another and another. This way you will be busy all through your life.

A constructively busy person has no time for gossip, blaming the government, idling away, wishing evil on others or being envious. You are just too busy creating your life that most irrelevant things do not matter to you. You are busy building your masterpiece as best as you can that you have little or no time for frivolities. Everything you do is deliberate. Spending time with friends and family, serving God, committing to a cause, ...everything, they are all deliberate. They must fit into your plan. By plan, I mean the master plan of your life. You do not leave anything to chance.

Now take a picture of that woman that is so busy you have to book an appointment to see her. When you are with her, she has little or no time that you have to go straight to the point and tell her what you are there for because if you waste her time, you know she may not give you audience another time. What do you think of this person you just pictured? It doesn't matter if she is a school teacher, bank executive, doctor, an entrepreneur and the likes, would you respect her or not? Would you value what she has to say or not? I believe you are beginning to get the picture.

So we have to at every point in time have worthy goals that not only benefit us but benefit society as well. When you are busy with them, you don't fall for everything or anything at all because you are so busy that you cannot entertain any distractions. In this state, this is only when you are in control. If you are not in control of your life, others will. And, when others control your life, you know what happens.

To be happy you need to be the scriptwriter as well as the director and producer of your life movie at the same time. The show is on, and you are the lead character in it. The world is watching. What exactly do you want them to see in this movie? What stories do you want to hear the audience saying about you as the lead character? Your answers to these questions and a little more will determine what you will write on the script of your life. Now go ahead write that script and start acting. Remember, there are no dress rehearsals when you make a mistake, rewrite the script and do better next time.

By this, you have accepted full responsibility for your happiness. Your happiness here is not in the hand of anyone; it is in your own hands. You have to plan for it. If you do not prepare for happiness, you will reap pain, anger, depression, frustration and so on. So you have to accept responsibility for your happiness and plan for it just like you are planning for everything in your life.

Remember, no one can make you feel unhappy or angry except

you give them the right to do that to you. If there is something that you still want from the other person, whether it is a job, love, respect or money, or even custody of children, the other person will control you with that thing you need. The moment you decide that you no longer want anything from the other person, you are free again. You have collected the power and the ability to control you from that person. Don't let anyone use anything to control you. Make up your mind that you can live without it and find other options or solutions. You can't be at the mercy of anyone. Seek alternatives all the time.

Determine to pay the price for happiness

There is always a price you will pay to be free from any unhappiness. There is always something that you need to start doing or stop doing to be free from unhappiness. If you search yourself sincerely, you know what the price is. The question now is, "Are you willing to pay the price?"

Before you respond, know that if you trade your peace of mind and happiness for anything you will end up without both.

Confront your problems and challenges. The more willing you are to confront the challenges, issues and difficulties you face every day, sincerely, the happier you will be.

Develop the habit of finding solutions at any given circumstance

Do not engage in self-pity, blaming, complaining, explaining, or whining. Get to work, fix the situation. As you continue to seek solutions and face your challenges sincerely and objectively evey day in every given case, it will become a part of you and the more strength, confidence as well as resilience you will have. You will stop being afraid of unpleasant situations or situations that seem difficult in your work and personal life. You will begin to deal with life as it is not as you wish it were.

I can't say this enough, "Challenges, problems and difficulties will be thrown at you every day". These are tests sent to you to test your character and readiness for the next stage. Welcome them! Just like conventional school, as you grow, the exams get more difficult. Even when you have re-sits, the re-sits are more difficult. Welcome them with gratitude so you can act with clarity and move to the next step. Once you accept that these challenges, problems and difficulties come to you to refine you and usher you into the next level, you will never have any prolonged moments of sadness anymore.

10

VITAL TO YOUR SUCCESS

Health

Attention to your health is highly essential. You cannot joke with it at all. You need your health to live to the fullest. If you are unhealthy in any way, this will affect your peace of mind. You will have to do all you have to do to make sure you are in excellent health every day.

If you achieve all kind of things in the material world, but you lose your health, you will get little or no satisfaction from your other accomplishments, because they will be useless to you. Thus the number one thing is your health to stay happy.

Relationships

Your success will depend on the people you associate with to a great extent. The more people you know; who positively know you, the more successful you will be at anything you attempt. One person, at the right time, in the right place, can open a door for you that can save you years of hard work and change your life forever. Thus it would help if you made conscious effort to build relationships. Your ability to form the right connections with the right people at every stage of your life will be pertinent to your success and determine how quickly you rise. Make a deliberate effort to start expanding professional contacts and friendships. Get involved with as many professional organisations and other bodies as you can and volunteer your services anytime you can. The more people you know and work with the more doors of opportunity will open up for you when the time is right.

When you meet people, communicate with them each time you find a good reason to interact with them. Don't waste their time by sending mundane stuff to them or keep sharing broadcast messages. They only have so much time, so don't waste it when you have the opportunity. Send something noteworthy, something you think they need; it could even be an invitation to an event you are organising. They may not respond, but your name is getting out little by little. The day you meet these persons you have something to open a conversation with, "... I sent a letter to your office last month, sent an invite, sent ..." you continue from there. Continue to sow seeds sooner or later your efforts will yield results.

Just like seeds, different contacts have different germination periods. So you must be patient as you continue to sow. Make it a habit and give of yourself without expectations. What goes around comes around, when you least expect, you will reap from sources you least expected.

At every point in life, someone is usually standing there guiding you in one direction or another. Every significant change in your life will be associated with a change in the people you live or work with at that moment. At every turning point, they are either opening or closing a door for you or helping you in some way; this is why you must carefully select the relationships you keep. You cannot afford to waste your precious time with people who are going nowhere in their lives. No matter how nice you think they are now, you can't risk your God-given destiny by hanging with them. You have to set high standards for your friends and associates and refuse to compromise. This is very important. Never joke with this. If you decide to compromise on this, your growth and development will be affected in a very serious way. There's more on this in the next chapter.

Bliss

Having peace of mind and staying at bliss always must be the central organising principle of your life. It should be your number one goal before anything else. You are only successful to the degree to which you can achieve your own internal happiness, your own contentment, your inner sense of personal well being – thus your inner peace of mind. If you don't commit to achieving your own happiness, no one else would. If your aim in life were only to make others happy, then you would be at the mercy of the feelings of others. You can't give what you don't have. You need to be in the right state first just as you can't help the poor by becoming poor yourself. You have to determine under what conditions it exists for you.

There are always going to be doubts, challenges, troubles, fears, disappointments, anger, worries, resentments, but determine to keep your inner peace in spite of these conditions. When you have learnt to have these situations under control, only then do you achieve total freedom and you have true power. People's actions don't get to you, and your happiness is not dependent on them. At this state, you are at peace. Any situation you find yourself you find the lessons or blessings in it and move on.

You need always to eliminate the negative people, situations and emotions that make you unhappy. Be detached from situations and people that threaten your peace of mind. There are two helpful ways you can handle any situation that is causing you stress or unhappiness. First, you can take action. You can move forward and do something to change the situation. You can equally assert yourself in the situation and make it different somehow. Secondly, you can simply walk away. You regain control by letting go of a person or situation and get busy doing something else.

In some instances, the very best thing you can do in a situation where you feel out of control is to leave the scene. When you leave, you regain control. Self-confidence comes with feeling in control; it is the reason why a person with clear purpose and a plan always has the edge over someone who is vague or unsure.

When you have placed inner peace as your overarching goal and plan everything you do in terms of whether it aligns or hinders your attainment of that goal, you will make better decisions as well as say and do the right things which are in alignment with your goals. At this level, you are not vulnerable to anyone, anything or any situation. You will find yourself operating from a position of strength, and you will feel wonderful about yourself.

Not until I found out how to make myself happy and be contented in myself I was never truly happy.

I went from being just ordinary to a certain level of comfort between 2008 and 2011. In 2012 I was going down. Then I didn't know what mattered. However, in 2015, February to be precise, I began building my life back. My journey of becoming a better me every day started. How did I do that? First, I took responsibility for my life and made a firm decision not to blame anyone nor any situation for my predicaments or challenges anymore. I became solutions oriented and began to sow in expectation of fruits. My life did a 360 degrees turn from this moment.

Today, I am happy in any situation. I am happy when I have many, and I am equally happy when I seem not to have much. If we look carefully, we always have tons of potentials within that we can explore to change any situation.

I worked in places where I got paid to barely live by and others I got fame and could relate with the crème de la crème of society, but all that ends when you quit the job because they were not true securities. Real security is the one you give yourself because it cannot be taken away. If you are disciplined and persistent, you will have all that you desire. Who are those people you want to relate with, what help can you provide to them? What problem can you solve for them? Once you answer these questions and get to work, you will get to where you want. And, remember in every situation, your happiness is of paramount importance — no kissing of asses; no walking on eggshells for any reason. You are charming, but you don't take your eyes off the ball. You have to do what you want to do and do it well. Even as you are charming, you need to be tough but fair in every given situation.

As you deliberately set peace of mind and inner bliss, as your organising principle, you become a more positive person. You become more relaxed and friendly with people. You thus accomplish much more than you ever could if otherwise. Without peace of mind, you cannot entirely focus on anything.

Forgiveness

To be truly happy, you must learn to forgive two persons. The first person you need to forgive is anyone who has hurt you in any way. Holding a grudge will hinder your progress; thus you need to forgive anybody that has hurt you. They are not worth your being angry or upset over whoever nor whatever they did. Whether they accept they are wrong or not, let it go. You have to let it go. Say you forgive them. Learn the lesson from the experience and move on. Use your energy for better things.

Life goes a lot smoother as you let go of the negative emotions and grudges. Even those who never said they were sorry to you, you have to forgive them. It may be hard at first, but one day you will wake up and find out that the pain doesn't hurt so much anymore. Eventually, the pain will go away completely.

The fact you forgive them doesn't mean you have to condone their actions. You don't have to invite them to dinner if you don't have to either. The reason you forgive them is actually a selfish one. It is to help you let go of any feelings of anger or resentment you may be feeling. It simply frees you from being a victim of those negative emotions. Besides, in no time you will find out they don't even matter at all. As you get busier in life, you have little or no space in your heart to think about what someone did or didn't do. You really don't give a damn anymore.

The second person you need to forgive is yourself. You may have done something you are not proud of, hurt someone who has refused to forgive you, behaved in a less than honourable way, whatever it is, now you feel guilt or shame or you feel both. You have to forgive yourself and let it go. What is done is done, you can't undo it. The shame and guilt are hindering your happiness. Let the guilt go! Let the shame go! Despise shame and banish shame. Do not let it affect your identity. You have to deal with it and let it go. If you need to apologise to anyone, go to the person to apologise or call them up to apologise. Then very important, apologise to yourself. Make your sincere apologies and close the chapter.

Your full-time job is to keep yourself happy rather than allowing anything to make you feel sad. You have to let go of any feelings of anger, guilt, shame and resentment towards yourself or anyone; this is crucial to your staying positive and happy.

Vocation

Your vocation is the platform through which your God-given potentials will be unveiled. It is an opportunity to transform your dreams into reality. Dreams without work accomplish nothing. Thus, you should see work as a blessing, not as a punishment. Your vocation will help you to stay active, build your self-esteem teach you some valuable lessons. As you advance in your work life, you will learn that the discovery and use of talents, skills and abilities are far more important than the acquisition of wealth. Your vocation will help you develop an attitude that sees a problem as a reason for celebration because, because within problems lie the possibility for success. It is also a platform to bless others and to unleash hidden potentials you never knew existed.

However, stay in the centre of what you love to do. When you are passionate, and you love what you are doing when it is what you want to do, not what you have to do, you always do it better because you are doing it with love.

Doing a job, you should do because of circumstances or refusal to stretch instead of doing what you love is leading a false life. Your job should be something you would do whether you were paid or not. When you enjoy your vocation you enjoy your life; the lines between work and play start to blur. Everything becomes a learning experience.

It always takes courage to do the thing you love and go against the majority. It also takes courage to resist the temptation to try to please others and be true to yourself. It isn't your responsibility to do anything to please anyone or prove to anyone; it is their job to work to please themselves and to find their own happiness.

This is your life, and you are the heroine in it; you must follow your own heart. I can't tell you what job to do, neither can anybody else. Only you have to figure that out by yourself. People can only make suggestions for you, but the decision is yours to make. If you look within you, you will definitely find answers.

Quit taking jobs because they will look good on your resume. Do only what you love. What you love may seem difficult to do, but at the end of the day, you will find out it was worth every bit of it.

Nevertheless, it is essential for your vocation to have some profitability. Never be blinded by strong love and forget you have to pay bills. Look within yourself and find how you can take what you are doing to the zenith. It requires you to work harder and risk more, but hard work always pays.

The heights by great men reached and kept were not attained by sudden flight, but they, while their companions slept, were toiling upward in the night. - Henry Wadsworth Longfellow

Courage

You require courage to be successful. Courage is needed to step out of your comfort zone; to overcome inertia and to face challenges.

Courage is also required to handle criticisms. The moment you become successful people are going to start talking about you and criticising you from every corner. Courage is needed to overcome the criticisms and critics.

You need the courage to step out of what you are used to into the unknown and stretch. No growth takes place without stretching. You need to stretch yourself to reach your highest potentials.

To succeed you are going to need to take risks, go on journeys you have never gone before, take paths you have never taken before, associate with people you have never seen before, enter into businesses you haven't done before, get into unfamiliar territories. You will have to stretch yourself and overcome fear to do all these things. The very act of doing something that is out of your comfort zone chases fear and doubt on the spot.

Courage also does not exist in the absence of fear of some danger. Being able to confront whatever is on your way and take action in spite of your fears is key to success. The only way to overcome every form of fear is to move toward it and address it head-on. As you move toward it, it grows smaller and more manageable; your fears begin to lose their control over you.

Once you are close to the source of your fear, you have to deal with it directly. Be willing to face situations or persons that cause you fear directly. Only then can you put the fear behind you. You will need the courage to face the fears. When you can force yourself to face any fear-inducing situation in life, your self-confidence gets a boost and so does your self-esteem, respect and personal pride.

Resolve today not to allow fear to make you unhappy for another minute. Pick the courage to confront every situation or person that causes you to fear and put it behind you. By continuously facing up to challenges, you eventually get to a point in life when you are afraid of nothing.

Know that, every crisis and problem you go through on the journey is designed to promote you. Challenges are divine announcements; you will soon outgrow your current situation. When a higher position comes, it's an indication that you will leave your comfort zone because to fit into that new position, you will do some stretching.

If you attain any position without stretching and going through the process first, you won't be able to keep the position. It's a simple law of nature. You cannot dodge it. You require courage to thrust into these unfamiliar territories and to pull through.

Here is a thing, after all is said and done, you will lament the chances you didn't take in life far more than you will your learning experiences (circumstances that appeared to be failures).

I believe the worst sin anyone can commit against nature is not using your potentials to make the world a better place. Not living to your potential is shortchanging yourself and robbing the world.

Someone needs the potentials you have buried inside you. The world needs the potentials you possess. I know this because you are a unique being. You have something within you that you do like no other one could. You know it within you. Find the courage to unleash these potentials. As you push past your comfort zone despite your fears, the fears lessen their grip on you and your courage expands.

Ultimately, what is going to make you happy is growth; this requires that you step out of your comfort zone now and then. As you continuously perform fearful acts, you will find that things you once thought were scary aren't as scary as they seemed.

Preparation also lessens fear and increases your courage. Prepare, prepare, prepare and prepare always. The more you prepare for your assignments, the less fear you will have.

As you become more confident in yourself and your abilities, you can set even larger goals. As time goes on, your doubts and fears will weaken, and your courage and confidence will become the dominant force that controls your actions. You will be able to face every situation with calmness and self-assurance.

Environment

The environments in which we live affect the nature of our living. The light that is continually surrounded by darkness is in danger of losing its brilliance. Plant yourself in an environment that keeps you motivated. Plant yourself in an environment that will propel you to succeed.

Determine your location. The kind of fish you want to catch determines if it's an ocean, river or lake you will go to as well as the tactics you will use. You can't want to catch a shark and go to a lake. The output you want will determine your location, approach, weapons and so on.

What you are exposed to is what you will retain and what you think about all the time. And, what you think about is what you will become. You can't picture what you have not seen or heard of before. What you see you replicate. You first have to see it before you can replicate the picture.

You need to deliberately plant yourself in environments that intimidate you and inspire you. Spend some time with great people, visit great places, attend great events, read great books and listen to great messages.

Knowledge

You need knowledge. It's absolutely necessary for you to be knowledgeable. You will need to study to become knowledgeable in different aspects. In your chosen career, know everything that you can learn. Some people say once you have money you don't need to have a university degree or masters and a PhD. Well, maybe you don't, but most of the people I have seen who didn't achieve a university degree spend most of their lives explaining to people why they didn't and justifying why they don't need it. Again, if it were to be the coolest thing to do, why do they send their kids to the best schools in the world? It is because deep down within them they know the value of education.

The first step is to get at least a university first degree. Schools set the foundation for your life; your character polishing process starts from schools. That is the foundation. Our parents are our first teachers they provide us with the tools we need in life then our teachers teach us how to use those tools. You will learn to be smart and how to relate with people. When you go to the best schools in the world, they will instill in you a mindset of being the best in the world. From there you will be exposed to other ideas.

Do not stop at the university degree. Develop the attitude of studying all the days of your life. When you study you learn and become smarter and smarter by the day. When you don't study and research, after a while, you begin to stink. You run out of ideas; your ideas become obsolete. You begin to repeat the same ideas and strategies you learnt years ago and by using the same ideas and strategies over and over again; you start to stink. When you are standing before someone who studies all the time, she finds you irritating. And, gradually people you thought you are in the same class will start avoiding you. You ask yourself "why are they leaving me". I will tell you why. It is because you have failed to update yourself continuously and have started stinking. You are now incompatible. They cannot cope with you anymore. You can never catch up with them by trying to convince them how good your friendship was. They have gone on to greater things because they deliberately seek knowledge every day, expose themselves to greater things, more opportunities and deliberately plant themselves in environments of success. They read, and they seek knowledge every day from books, films, audios and things around them. They improve who they are, what they do, what they have every day. They don't settle! The moment you start settling, you start becoming archaic.

For you to move ahead, you have to keep learning. You can go no further with your current level of knowledge and skills. Your advancement will depend on what you learn and practice to a great extent. Continuously update, update, update and update your reservoir of knowledge.

When you become very knowledgeable in any area, you become more competent and confident in that area. And when you are very competent and confident in any field, the more returns you will get from that field. Seek to be the best at what you do. When you are the best at what you do, or if you have a solution to a problem, the world will beat a path to your doorstep. It doesn't matter if you are black, white, green or from the moon or mars.

As you seek knowledge, you will be exposed to more opportunities, and you will be exposed to other like-minded people.

Develop the habit of reading at least an hour or two every day. Listen to audio tapes, listen to motivational speakers, and watch films that inspire you. As you do all these, you will become more knowledgeable, competent and confident.

Most situations I go through in life, one way or another I have come across similar situations or advice for such situations either in a book, broadcast, movie, relations with others and in seconds, I just know what to do. Someone has done it with these results so let me try it this way. Sometimes when I begin to tell you how a scenario will play out, you would think I am a psychic. Well, I get the ideas from my repertoire of knowledge nothing else.

As you continue to seek knowledge, your subconscious also starts coming to your aid. You will start finding answers to questions in different things, even in your dreams and flashes. You may be looking for a way to solve a problem, and as you tune on your TV, you find your answer, or you see a movie that directs your path, or you may instinctively open to a page in a book that will contain the answers. Thus every day, dedicate time to read or listen to messages.

You can't afford to be outdated. You need to update your knowledge base continuously.

Knowledge is for you to use not to prove

Another part of seeking knowledge is that it is for your personal development, your purpose and your future. It is not for you to prove to anyone that you have the knowledge. Definitely what you know will set you apart but never brag about it or use it to feel superior. You are just you. You are not superior to anyone, and no one is superior to you at the same time because you are a unique being.

Bragging about what you know or trying to prove to people is immaturity. It is immaturity of the highest order. It means you are still at the kindergarten level in the school of excellence.

By bragging and proving or showing, people will begin to resent you. What you know should help make the world a better place not for you to offend people or drive people away from you.

Seek to improve who you are, what you do, what you know every day for you and to help people and to make the world a better place. As a radical being, you must help make a difference in the world through the things you do and to help make the world a better place.

11

ASSOCIATION

*T*he top five people you relate with mostly in your life will give a reflection of who you are and what you will become. You will have to manage the choice of people you associate with, as much as you can. If you sleep with dogs, you will wake up with fleas. When you move with bad people unconsciously, you will start picking up their habits and acting like them. You will talk like them, walk like them, make decisions like them and behave like them. You may not notice the transition, but in no time you will begin to pick these characters gradually and start acting them out. The reverse is also true for when you associate with good people. If you surround yourself with caring, trustworthy, honest, positive, goal-oriented people, their positive charge will motivate and inspire you. Their optimism will be contagious.

Always deliberately strive to associate with people who inspire you; people who make you want to be better. Believe it or not, the people you allow into your life will ultimately have the most significant impact on your attitude.

Soar with the eagles and be like them. Move with champions and become one. If you are in an association with five wise people, you will become the sixth wise person, and if you are associating with five fools, you will become the sixth fool. The decision is yours.

You will need to stay away from negative people and those who drag you down. Please do not such people to be a part of your life, because, anybody who makes you feel worthless, anxious or uninspired is poisoning your software and wasting your precious time. Continually hanging with them, they will start making you more like them, and you will start acting like them. Please, life is too short to be in a union with people like this. Flee from them! Cut them loose! They are nothing but trouble.

Sometimes also as you get busy improving your life, you find you outgrowing your close friends. You no longer think alike or have the same values. Gradually, you start growing apart and become incompatible. I have experienced this time and time again. Dear friend, do yourself a favour move on and start spending your time with those you have the same testimonies and have a similar purpose with yours. Love the old friends from afar. If you don't let go of people who don't fit anymore, the ones that fit won't come in. To meet new and exciting people, you have to stop associating with the old group.

Quality Relationships

As you start getting successful, you also start becoming like a magnet. Your aura changes and people start getting glued to you like bees. At this point, you get to choose those you want to be part of your tribe.

Remember, your friends influence everything you do consciously and unconsciously. Thus, you will need to watch the people you hang around.

Inaction and indecisiveness and acting like you are scared or to be pitied are the quickest ways to chase people away from you. Walk and act like you know where you are going; people will gravitate towards you and follow you.

- Accept others unconditionally. Everybody is unique. You are who you are they are who they are. You can only change yourself; you can't change anyone.

- Earn trust by being trustworthy. Keep your word all the time. Your word is your bond.
- Do nice things without expecting anything in particular in return.
- Be loyal, even when it may not be the popular thing to do. Loyalty is a two-way street. When you give you get.
- Listen to others not to judge them but to understand their point of view.

Build a Reservoir of Goodwill

Create a human environment in which you can be happy, contented and fulfilled. You must examine your relationships, one by one and develop a plan to make each of them enjoyable and satisfying.

No one works for free. There is always a hidden motivation. Always ask yourself in given situations, "what you are going to give to get them to help you." The most successful people in our society, in all fields of endeavour, are those who have helped a vast number of other people to achieve the things they want. They build a reservoir of goodwill and create a propensity in others to help them, to reciprocate for having been helped in the past.

Your returns in life come back to you as a result of your contribution to others. If you take every opportunity that you can to help others, others will eventually give you all the help you need.

If you sow hard work, helpfulness and honesty, you will get back riches, rewards and the respect of other people.

The Golden Rule

Do unto others as you would have them do unto you. Treat other people as though they are the most important people in the world. Tennis Champion Roger Federer once said, "It's nice to be important, but it's more important to be nice." Strive to be nice to people. Sometimes it's very hard, I know, but try your best to be. I'm trying my best too in this regard. I've come to understand that, you can never find true happiness when you mistreat others. When you mistreat others, the universe will send it back to you; this is because the energy that you put out into the world comes back to you. Everybody is special. God put them on the planet for a reason. When you are kind, you will reap kindness from the universe. Your behaviour will either propel you forward in the quest for your dreams or take you backwards. Thus it's up to you to decide what to do.

It was Mary Kay Ash I believe that said "everyone is wearing a sign on their neck that says "make me feel important". If you would be honest with yourself, you seem to gravitate towards those friends that treat you like somebody important to them. In one's growing years, you may suck up to some people who treat you like trash because you thought they were important or had something you wanted. But when you get beyond that stage and you know you possess all you need, permit me to use the f-word you say "f…them" That is when you begin to reflect and remember A was good to me, B was good to me C, Oh no, best he or she is in his or her corner. That's how it goes.

Every day in every way, look for ways to help other people to do their jobs better and live better. This will build up a vast reservoir of positive feeling toward you that will boomerang and come back to you later in life.

Some toxic people to Avoid

Negative people are usually the primary cause of most unhappiness in our daily interactions. You have to cut them loose. Staying in a bad relationship can be enough in itself to cut short your full potential for success and happiness. There is no suggestive influence more powerful than the people around you. Choose them with care. The following are some of those you should flee from; I've described them to some degree so you can recognise them when you see them.

The Dumpers

Some people always run to you to dump their problems on you. They dump it on you and go home to sleep. You are not responsible for other people's business. You have to set up boundaries. Like a business, you have to have hours of operation.

Say "I'm open for business from this time to this time" and don't pick up the phone or respond to their messages when you are not open.

Alarmists

Some other people are alarmists who come to steal your peace. Everything is a great problem. So much drama! The help did something wrong; it's a major issue. A friend did something to them; it's a major issue.

Every little thing they run to you to save them. Well, you can't carry everyone's burden just as you can't fix everyone. Some people don't want to change. They just love the attention their problems bring. Please, don't feel guilty when you cannot assist.

In life, you are going to encounter a couple of them. Once you recognise them, seize giving them the time of day. Concentrate on running your race. Be so focused on your race to have no time to look around.

I can't warn you enough; by keeping them happy, you will make yourself sad and lose focus on your goals. You don't have the energy to keep them happy. Look for happy friends that will inspire you. If you don't remove the wrong people from your life, the right people won't come in. You have to set boundaries for these peace stealers.

Your number one priority is to keep yourself happy. If you try to fix everyone you can't be happy. There will always be people who want something from you. They might be good people but don't let them affect you with their worries, doubts and negativity. Put your feet down and do what you have to do to remain steadfast in achieving your goals.

Relationships are built on two-way streets. They have to be mutually beneficial. Each side has to bring something valuable to the table; otherwise, they will not endure. You cannot be the only one inspiring people all the time. If you allow that, you will get drained and become sad. Let them know they are responsible for their lives and their actions. Let them grow up and look elsewhere to solve their problems. They don't need your advice. They should get on with their lives and leave you to get on with yours.

I once had a friend I would call Helen; everything is a big problem for her. So much drama surrounds everything. Wants to get married today, tomorrow, next tomorrow, and so on! Different stories and issues every day but they are usually not true or relevant. All she wants is to get attention; something for her to be talking about to feel relevant.

It went on and on. Every day she would make up new stories to have something to talk about; to make you believe she has this new plan for advancing her life. I talked and talked and talked but every time we were always back at the same bus stop. Then one day I stopped talking. On one occasion, I was at her apartment she said to me "Keno I have been talking for two hours you haven't uttered a word", I said, "I'm listening to you". She kept pressing I still didn't respond to what she wanted me to respond to. About a week later, she visited me at my apartment, and I did the same thing to her, and she left. "But did she stop? No! She changed her strategies.

They always seek new ways to get to you because they are too idle and have all the time to conceive funny ideas to get your attention. They could buy you all kinds of gifts do the unimaginable for you just to keep you as a spectator in their lives; but realise that they are only after one thing, your attention. And, you cannot give them that attention they desire and still accomplish your goals.

With my "ex-friend," this continued for over two years until I set up boundaries; she didn't find it funny. Kept calling and calling but I had moved on. She still tries every once in a while, but now I have a "do not disturb sign" on my door.

Some other time, another lady like Helen was coming very close to me in another area I lived. The moment I recognised the traits, I took to my heels. She was always complaining about how she was in this mess or in that mess, grand plans today, other great plans tomorrow no action on anyone. Hmmm! We don't have the energy to keep anyone happy. We also do not have the strength and time to help anyone who does not want to be helped to straighten her life. When you recognise them, kiss and say goodbye, no good will come out of it.

The Soap Opera Stars

Some don't need your help but they are people who think life is one big soap opera and they are the stars in it. They often have over the top attitudes. They could be charming, charismatic, narcissistic, flamboyant, imaginative, compelling and persuasive. They love drama and love being in the spotlight. They assign your role either as one of the supporting cast, or an extra put on the set to serve as a fool to their whims and fancies. They need spectators; you are their spectator.

The curtain never comes down. Their lives are long-running series. Just when you think the end is near, they create another drama. They are control freaks, and you are the puppet they are stringing along.

To validate their own lives, they need you around as a witness – not as a participant or a loveable sidekick, just a witness. As soon as you try to get a speaking part, they step on your lines.

If you are smart, you need to head for the exit. Tell them you will gladly read the reviews, but you don't have time for another opening or another show.

12

SOME TRUTHS ABOUT YOUR JOURNEY

Seasons of Insignificance

Until you have moved some distance, you will appear to be insignificant. Don't be discouraged. You are a diamond in the rough. You are in your preparatory stage. You may seem insignificant for a while but when you get unleashed it will be a divine announcement to the world.

Seasons of Waiting

Expect to spend some time waiting; because everything worthwhile takes time. You will spend a good amount of time to plant and more time waiting for your fruits to mature and be harvested. But, trust me, it's going to be worth it.

It takes a shorter time to build a bungalow than it takes to build a skyscraper. The bungalow owner will start and finish his building when the skyscraper is still in foundation stage. The skyscraper will take even ten times longer time to be completed but when the skyscraper is completed the bungalow owner will be looking up to the skyscraper.

Seasons of Isolation

When your purpose on earth is about to be revealed, you are placed in a place of aloneness.

The road to outstanding success is a lonely road. You will find yourself alone so many times; sometimes by design sometimes by circumstances. This is very vital to your growth. It is at these periods of aloneness that unique ideas are born.

At this place, so many things happen to you. This usually precedes your movement from one level to another level. Most times circumstances throw you into a place of isolation to get you to reflect. You can't help it, you just find yourself there. It is essential when you are at this place of aloneness to maintain a positive attitude and reflect.

However, you will need to spend time alone deliberately; quality time alone away from the world to get intimate with yourself. You have to do this for your deliberate advancement. Isolation presents a chance to draw upon who you are, your strengths and your untapped potentials. This is when you reflect on your entire life and make decisions on the way forward.

You need alone time to reflect on your past present and your future. At this place of uninterrupted introspection, you see yourself clearly in relation to life. There are people who never have the chance in their "busy people" lives to meditate, to ponder their mistakes or to examine the direction their lives are taking. Without these reviews, stagnation sets in and personal growth is stunted. But, when you withdraw for a moment alone while reflecting you become self-aware as you engage in self-identity search. This can be an invigorating experience as it gives you an opportunity to reinvent yourself if need be and launch a brand new you.

Isolation gives you the opportunity to think about yourself, your life, what things mean to you, what your options are and new possibilities. At this quiet space that surrounds you, you get new thoughts and new insights as well as a strong sense of self. You get a chance to reflect on perspectives you may never have the opportunity to look at in the presence of others.

Turning your back on the Crowd

The majority will always conform to get acceptance, but if you want to lead the orchestra, you've got to turn your back on the crowd. Most successful people forge ahead moments other people waste because they have learned how to be alone. They get productive during their alone time.

Moments of Doubt

Expect moments where you will question your ability to achieve your dream. Sometimes it may seem to be in vain but don't give up. In those moments of doubt, focus your attention on the very next step you need to take. Take your thoughts from the whole journey and focus on just the next step, and the next and the next. One step at a time is all that every successful person took.

Sometimes your assignment may look small, but it may be a means to another opportunity. When you perform faithfully well in this assignment, you will be plunged into a higher opportunity. Distractions and delays will come now and then but don't give up. The results of keeping steadfast will be immense.

Moments of Weakness

Some days you will feel tired, discouraged, under the weather, or lacking energy, that's when doubts set in. At these moments, remind yourself that everyone on earth has these moments, but it is a question of management. Are you going to let how you are feeling stop you? My guess is no. Know that these situations are temporary and they will pass. Endeavour to do something that will make you happy every day. When you are happy, your belief will be strong. With every experience as you take steps, your belief will increase and strengthen. You will discover who you are and what you are truly capable of on earth.

Likes Attract Likes

More often than not, you attract into your life people and situations in harmony with your dominant thoughts. Everything you see in your life, you have attracted to yourself because of the person you are, primarily because of your dominant thoughts.

The more you desire or fear something, the more likely you are to attract it into your life. A thought without an emotion behind it has no power to influence you one way or the other. Keep your thoughts on the things you want and keep them off the things you fear.

Nothing around you has any connotation except the connotations you give to it with your thoughts, if you change your ways of thinking, you change your life. This is because your dominant thoughts will be manifested.

Your family, your relationships, your friends, your job, your problems and your present opportunities, have all been attracted to you because of the way you think of them.

Birds of the same feather flock together. You will tend to meet and become involved with people and situations that are vibrating in harmony with your dominant thoughts and emotions.

As you look around you at every aspect of your life, positive or negative, you will see that your entire world is of your own making. And, the more emotion you attach to a thought, the greater will be the rate of vibration and the more rapidly you will attract people and situations in harmony with that thought into your life.

Being clear about what you want, and the kind of people you want to be associated with, you will draw them into your life.

Everything you see around you began as a thought or an idea in the mind of one person before it was translated into reality. Everything concerning your life started first as a thought, a wish, a hope, or a dream either in your mind or in someone else's mind. Your outer world ultimately becomes a manifestation of your inner world and reflects back to you what you think about most of the time.

Successful people think about what they want, and how to get it most of the time.

Your thoughts are a form of energy that vibrates at a speed determined by the level of emotional intensity accompanying the thoughts. When you are excited, you attract people, more situations and actions that will be consonance with that state of mind.

It is true that happy people seem to attract other happy people. Active people attract other active people into their lives. A person with a prosperity mindset appears to attract people with similar mindsets. Hence, you need to deliberately control your thoughts to focus on what you want and refusing to think about what you don't want.

Expect the best of yourself. The great philosopher Goethe said, "One must be something to be able to do something." You have to change yourself to become a different person on the inside before you can see different results on the outside. You can't fake what you are not for very long. Before long, the real you is exposed. People can smell your level of confidence from afar. They can tell from the way you talk, walk and other little mannerisms. Also if what you are on the inside is not from within, when the external factor that gave you that personality is removed you become exposed and become vulnerable. You lose your acquired superficial confidence.

Stepping Out of Your Comfort Zone

Life begins at the end of our comfort zone only by stretching we get there. Where there is no struggle, there is no growth. Most progress we make in life come as a result of stretching experiences.

You may think the journey to success is too complicated; what's the point you may ask. Well, I will tell you that, first and foremost you have something within you that the world needs. Don't let it die with you. Secondly, if you choose mediocrity or living less than is possible over being the best that you can be, I bet you will be unhappy all your life. How do I know this? Because you are a radical being. You have so much within you waiting to be unleashed. How do I know you are a radical being? Because you have read this far. The others will not read this far. They will probably stop at the title or first page. But, you have read this far because you want more, you want to be a 'better you.'

If you are the smartest in a pack, get out of there. You don't belong there. Go to a group where you can learn.

Risk Taking

You must be willing to leave behind what feels familiar, safe and secure. Those who find security don't get it. Success and security belong to the risk takers. Why because they know security is a mirage. Successful people are risk takers. They are addicted to new. They want more, a new life, new challenges...name it. They want to get up and go, and that's one of the reasons they are successful.

More risks mean more experiences for you, and you will learn faster and better. Your range of experiences will be greater than you can imagine.

Controlling Your Outcomes

There are specific causes for everything that happens in our lives. This applies to success and failure as well. There are specific causes of success, and there are specific causes of failure. If you desire specific results, in your life that you want more of, you trace the results to the roots and repeat the process, although, sometimes there are reformed processes you can apply. Likewise, if you find situations in your life that you do not like, go to the roots, and get rid of them.

The change in your outer experience will also follow the change in your inner experience. The further you think into the future, the better decisions you will make in the present to assure that that the future becomes a reality.

If you sow the right causes, you reap the desired outcomes. If you produce quality products or services that people want and need and are willing to pay for and then promote them vigorously, you will be successful in selling them. If you don't, you won't. If you treat people nicely, they will be endeared to you, treat them poorly, they will avoid you.

The Principle of Sowing and Reaping

Every seed produces a harvest; good or bad. What you sow you will reap. The quality of your seeds will determine the quality of your harvests. Exceptional seeds will create exceptional yields.

Every day you ought to sow something. There should never be a day you have nothing to sow. If you sow nothing, your seed is nothing, and you will reap a season of nothing. If you sow gossip, you will reap a season of trouble. If you sow good seeds, you will reap a season of good rewards. If you sow bountifully, you will reap bountifully.

Every day you are sowing. How do you spend your time? Are you wasting it or investing it into a good cause that will yield beautiful rewards?

You need to plant seeds on the ground to get harvests. Sow amazing seeds every day to expect amazing opportunities every day. It is only by sowing every day you can expect rewards and blessings every day.

The seed you plant will, first of all, die before it will grow and get to maturity. Also, some seeds take longer time than others; for instance, the Chinese bamboo will take about six years of watering before it will sprout, but when it does, it grows to an unimaginable height within weeks. Likewise the cocoa plant; you spend years tendering, but when it starts bearing fruits you don't need to water anymore because the roots have grown very deep. And, you just keep collecting fruits.

The quality of the seed you plant and the time it takes before maturity will always determine the nature and quality of your harvest. When you increase the size of your seed, you will increase the size of your harvest. An uncommon seed will also always create an exceptional yield.

When you sow nothing you reap a season of nothing; sow bountifully to reap bountifully.

Instinct

Instinct takes you to success. Always listen to what your instinct places in your heart. Poverty and failure come when you decide to disobey your instincts. The universe will send you ideas, solutions at exactly the right time through different avenues. When you get these nudges, act on them immediately. If you get the urge to call someone or say something or do something and it feels right, obey your instincts. It will always turn out to be the right thing to do. Even when you have acted in faith, and it felt like it was a mistake, on the long run, you will realise that perceived mistake was consequential in taking you to exactly where you are supposed to be.

Where you are now, or where you are coming from doesn't matter, it is where you are going to that is most important.

Mastering the Art of Conversation

You have to learn the art of conversation. Your mouth runs your entire life. Losses or gains are a product of your mouth. Anywhere you are going to; there will be a word path. You talking to you, you talking to others, and you talking to God, there is a word path. What you tell yourself and what you tell people that you come in contact with, determine how far you will go. Someone has to like you first to show you favour, give you a job, buy from you, open up to you, and share ideas with you. The words from your mouth tell a lot about you and will determine to a large extent how much people will relate with you.

There may be some people the universe has placed in your path to impact your life, but they haven't because you haven't told them what they want to hear. They have to hear the words they want to hear from you first. This could be as a result of the fact that you are still being tested in the art of conversation. Focus, learn, pass the test and move to the next stage.

In conversations with yourself, tell yourself only positive things and in speaking to people, seek to speak only meaningful stuff to people.

Everyone can master the art of conversation. I'm learning to improve my conversational skills every day as well. I'm not perfect yet but I'm conscious, and I keep working at it every day. When you say what you shouldn't have, don't flog yourself too much, simply charge yourself to do better next time.

When with people, ask questions. When you ask the questions, you determine the quality of your conversations with people. Be careful too not to sound like an interviewer. Trust your instincts. Ask relevant questions that you genuinely want answers to, to keep the conversation going.

People will look at beauty, but they give their hearts to conversations.

The God Factor

The sower sows and waters but only God guarantees a harvest. Listen to that inner voice for advice always. That voice will guide you in sowing what He desires you to sow, and he will bless you accordingly. Listen to him, so you don't plant in vain.

When God begins to speak to you, he activates your vision. Never limit Him to your country alone to get harvests. Your harvests can come from anywhere in the world.

Whatever is for you is drawn to you.

The Luck Factor

There is luck, and there is no luck. To receive luck, you have to set the atmosphere or conditions to receive luck. If you are not set, you won't know what to do.

You are as lucky as to how hard you work. There are no two ways about it. Without putting yourself out there or doing the needful, you will not meet with opportunities. Imagine a junkie that takes drugs and spends her time sleeping or staying in that euphoric state every day, what are her chances of landing luck. Except if you say "she can get lucky getting more drugs from friends". Maybe that's true, but first, she was a junkie before getting that ill luck that will destroy her the more.

Luck is something that you can create. It is your ability to take advantage of opportunities you meet with. A simple equation usually used in books, **Luck = Preparation + Opportunity.**

You increase your luck probabilities by becoming an attractive force for luck to find you. This means, you need to cast your nets more often and in different waters to increase your chances. Again, you need to make the right decisions every time you meet an opportunity.

In essence, you need to be ready for luck. If you are not prepared, you may not even recognise it when it comes. You need to be more aware of all the chance opportunities available to you. This will help you to identify them.

You also need to make use of every good opportunity that comes to you. You can't afford to be lazy. The more you latch onto opportunities, the more opportunities that will find you. If you don't use them, they will seize to come. The secret thus is in the doing. As you take advantage of one opportunity and get to work, a new opportunity will develop from the one you are at, and even more, will keep coming up. Thus, you need to learn how to make intelligent and quick decisions.

To increase your chances, you need to relate more with people and be friendlier. Always help people when you can. Others too will be willing to help you. It's called the "boomerang effect". Everything you do will come back to you one day.

Furthermore, you will need to increase your intuition. To increase your intuition, it means you have to use it every time it sends you a message. If you don't use it, you lose it. And, by using it more and more often, you increase it as it gets sharper and sharper. Every successful person you see has a strong sense of intuition. The more you use it and the more you are exposed to, the more intuitive you will become. The more you are able to trust your intuition and use it, the more success you are going to have in all areas of your life. You will be able to conceive more ideas and meet with more opportunities.

In addition, always be in a state of bliss. Never let anything affect your peace of mind. The moment something touches your peace of mind, you lose focus, and once you lose focus, you don't see any opportunities or recognise potential opportunities when they come. Like Rhonda Byrne said, "Miracles happen in a state of bliss". Thus protect your inner peace always. Engage in things that will make you feel at bliss every day. By the law of attraction, staying at bliss will attract more bliss.

If you would do all these things, you will be the luckiest person in the world.

Wherever Your Mind Goes, the Energy Goes

Wherever your attention goes, your life goes also. When you focus on a significant goal, you activate some unseen forces that will help you achieve that goal faster. You will find yourself in conversations about that specific object of your desire. You will receive information from different sources unexpected. It will appear as if you are surrounded by ideas and information that can be helpful to you in achieving your desires. You will suddenly begin to identify different opportunities and possibilities around you that have to do with achieving your desire.

Tests of Character

Whenever you are about to move to another level or another facet of you is to be revealed, you will pass through tests. These tests come in the form of problems. As you solve these problems, another facet of you is exposed.

You will face difficult challenges. Sometimes, they are extremely difficult situations. But, never be afraid of the challenges. What you are going through may have broken you down, but you are torn to grow back stronger. It's a process to prepare you for the next level. The process instills in you a particular strength of character and determination that will sustain you through every obstacle to fulfill your purpose.

Every obstacle or challenge transforms you to acquire the skills and abilities to overcome the obstacle or challenge. These skills and abilities shape you into the person you need to become to live the life of your dreams. Without acquiring the required skills, you won't be able to handle success; success will come to you and go down the drain as quickly as it happened.

Focus on passing the test. If you fail the test, you will have to, and the next test is always more difficult than the former. Thus never be upset about a situation. See them as tests of your character to take you to the next level. When you have passed the test, you become better and stronger than you were before the test.

The harder the battle, the greater the win. If you are living a normal life, you will face crises every two to three months. As you grow, your challenges increase to weekly, daily and per minute. You are given more problems to solve; from one to the other, to the other just like that.

Remember, the problem you are going through is to introduce you to another part of you. When a new part of you (potential, opportunity) is about to be revealed, it is presented to you through a problem. In solving the problem the new part of you is exposed. You discover the hidden potentials and opportunities.

When you start getting king-sized problems weekly, daily, per minute and per second, know that you have reached the place called "there."

Have a possible mindset that problems are nothing more except to introduce you to yourself. No adverse situations can be totally negative. Every negative circumstance also contains something good buried within the seemingly bad situation. Life isn't about the negative events you come across every day; it's about what you do with the golden opportunities hidden within. When you have passed the tests, you move to the next level.

The Birthing Pains

It is almost as if the universe gives you a final test just before you arrive at your destination. The struggles at this stage can be likened to birthing pains that occur just before the child is born. When the labour pains get so intense; this is an indication that the child is about to come into this world. So also in this process, it is when you are going through your most challenging learning experiences that you must channel your energies to control your thoughts and accept that the pressing challenge you are facing is only a part of the process that will ultimately bring you through to your goal.

Welcome the hurdles

Don't let the hurdles deter you; welcome them. The universe sets up these series of hurdles, or learning experiences, to train you in exactly what you need to learn. If you do not learn the lessons, whether it's in relationships, in business, in academics, with money or with your health, the universe will send you back through the learning experiences over and over again until you finally get it and learn what you are meant to learn. Then and only then, will you be allowed to proceed to the next level in your development.

Nobody has charmed you or cast a spell on you, it's all for your good. As a matter of fact you should be worried if there are no tests for over a prolonged period; because no test means no promotion.

Trust Your Superconscious Mind

You will begin to achieve great things only when you start trusting entirely in your superconscious mind. If you don't use it, you will lose it. Seek within every obstacle or disappointment you face the lesson or blessing in it.

As you keep trusting and using your superconscious mind, the more accelerated will be your growth. Expect more tests as you grow, and as you pass these tests, you will continue to find answers everywhere you look.

Tapping into this source, sometimes words will fall out of your mouth that will turn out later to have been exactly the right thing to say at the time. Your actions will fit a pattern consistent with what you ought to do and where you ought to be. Even some of your actions that appeared to be mistakes will turn out to be just what was the right thing to do at the time; because the journey that those mistakes take you through, plunge you onto a higher level of growth.

These coincidences will start happening repeatedly as you grow in your level of awareness. You will experience synchronicity of events and experiences aimed towards moving you towards your goals. Coincidences related to your thoughts and situations start occurring more frequently. You will have the urge to call someone, and the person will call you. Sometimes, you will get an urge to buy a book or a tape, to telephone or visit someone, to write a letter or make a decision that later turns out to be exactly the thing for you to do at that moment. You will pick up a book or magazine or open it to the exact page that has the answer you need. You need money for a project, and miraculously the money will come to you.

Nothing happens by chance. You attracted each and every one of these events to yourself through your thoughts. Any thought, plan, goal or idea you hold continuously in your conscious mind will be brought into reality by your superconscious mind. Same way you attract good things to you, you can attract bad things too if you dwell on them thus discipline your mind to only think of the things you want. Spend every minute of every hour of everyday thinking about your goals and desires. Think about good things like health, happiness, wealth and refrain from dwelling on what you do not want to see manifested in your life.

Crises Are Inevitable

Crises are life's wake-up calls. If you are living a busy life, you will keep experiencing crises. You will experience business crises, family crises, health crises, relationship crises and other crises. The problems and crises never stop. They keep coming from different angles. But, you control how you respond to them. Are you going to wallow in self-pity or take action? How you respond to them will determine your success.

13

MORE TRUTHS ABOUT YOUR JOURNEY

The Ideal Life

The ideal life is super focused, purposeful, positive and orderly so that you are moving toward goals that are important to you every minute of every hour of every day. You always know what you are doing and why you are doing it. You have a continual sense of forward motion; always on the move. You feel like a winner most of the time. The thrill of achieving your desire and the feeling of having overcome adversity and won through, against all the odds, gives you a sense of pleasure and excitement that can come from no other source. You get to a point where you can hardly wait to get up from bed in the morning, and you hate to go to bed at night. Because there are so many exciting things you need to do. Twenty four hours are no longer enough to take care of all you have to. You become so positive and self-confident that your friends barely recognise you.

In this state, you feel in control of your life because you have a clear purpose and a plan that you are consistently working with every day. This sense of control is the foundation for building greater happiness and success in the future.

Excellence

If you want to make a change in the world, you need to take a look at yourself. You have to change yourself first. And you need to start learning how to live in integrity. Be fully committed to excellence. It makes your future crave your presence. It increases with integrity. Be determined to make anything given to you better and improved. Don't let things die in your hands. Strive to be relevant. What is not used is discarded. The evidence of mediocrity is the resentment of excellence. Manipulators give gifts to control decisions while integrity gives gifts to reward excellence.

Excellence will always pay off at the end of the day. It takes you places you will never imagine. Keep your commitments and respect the time of others by not inconveniencing them.

Determine never to waste people's time in conversations. Go straight to the point always because genuinely successful people are very busy people. They want to finish with you quickly and move to the next item on their agenda.

Your excellent character will speak for you. People notice more than you will ever know. Even the universe does, and she rewards your efforts accordingly.

Living in Alignment with Your Values

You experience the highest level of happiness when what you are doing on the outside is in congruence with your values on the inside. When you are living in complete alignment with what you consider to be good and right and true, you will automatically feel happy and positive about yourself and your world.

We experience bliss when we are living in harmony with our innermost convictions and values. Living in alignment with our true values is the key to self-confidence, self-respect, and personal pride.

Know who you are, be clear about what you believe in and what you stand for. Know that, when you can't change people you can change "you." By changing you, I mean your response.

Overcoming Inertia

The most difficult mental obstacle you have to overcome is inertia, the tendency to slip back into your comfort zone and to lose your momentum.

All growth and progress require you to move out of your comfort zone in the direction of something bigger and better. You can only experience success and happiness when you are willing to look stupid, feel out of place and uncomfortable during the process of creating a new comfort zone at a higher level of effectiveness.

You have to deliberately extricate yourself from familiar territories and move upward and onward toward ever higher levels of accomplishment.

Being afraid doesn't accomplish anything. Rational fears keep us alive; step out and learn to make your fears work for you.

Anything worth doing is worth doing poorly at first

Whenever you start something new, expect to feel clumsy and awkward at first. You will feel inadequate and inferior, silly, and embarrassed but this is the price you pay to achieve excellence in everything you do. As you keep at it every day, you will become better. Determine to make your today better than yesterday and your tomorrow better than today. The more you practice what you learn in any field, the better, more confident, competent and skilled you will become in that area. You don't have to be the fastest or smartest. You only need tenacity. As long as you have that, you will excel.

The Perfection Trap

Some people get caught in the perfection trap. Nothing is ever good enough. They wait for all conditions to be perfect. News flash "Perfection is an illusion". Nothing is ever perfect; there will always be something, one little thing that will make things less than perfect. No matter how hard you try. The perfect technology today will be ousted by a new technology tomorrow. The perfect book today will not be perfect tomorrow because a better book will emerge. The perfect dress today won't be tomorrow. That perfect human being still has some faults. That perfect man or woman you see may have little or no scruples. What does this mean? No one is perfect.

Decide to accept where you are at and what you have as perfect no matter what anyone says or thinks. Accept that nothing is permanent and always have the belief this one is okay for now, the next one will be better. Do these to help you move ahead. After you have done your best, do not lie there condemning what you have done. Be proud of this one and tell yourself the next one will be better. With this kind of mindset, you will be able to overcome the perfection trap.

Trust me when you are at the *perfection bus stop*, you don't move forward. You remain on one spot. Do not let this happen to you.

Self Assessment

You need to examine yourself regularly to see if you are headed in the right direction. Failing to review your life periodically is a sure way to mediocrity. There's no growth without careful examination. Thus, you need to continually evaluate yourself through great questions and decide to be better. Every time you carry out an evaluation on yourself, you are going to have conversations with yourself, and out of these conversations will emerge change, great ideas and perceptions.

Failing Forward to Success

The best things in life don't come easily. A sailor doesn't learn from calm waters. We have to make mistakes occasionally; hence life wouldn't be fun. Accept them and learn from them.

It wouldn't be any fun if we didn't make mistakes. If I went out and played golf and every one of the eighteen holes I hit a hole in one, I wouldn't be playing golf for very long; I mean, you have to go into the rough occasionally to make the game interesting. Not too often though. - Warren Buffet

For a successful person, there is nothing like a failure. Every experience that appears like a setback or failure is actually a learning experience. Hence they embrace them and chew them for breakfast. The crucibles of life are but the touchstones for our growth.

Anything worth doing is worth doing poorly at first. Accept you are going to have to make mistakes. You are going to face setbacks. You will get frustrated sometimes. However, understand that the other side of frustration lies success.

Great success is often preceded by great learning experiences. Someone asked Thomas Edison once how he felt to have failed ten thousand times before creating the light bulb; he responded thus "I haven't failed; I have just found ten thousand ways that won't work."

You will never experience true success until you learn to embrace learning experiences. Nobody is perfect; we all make mistakes; I have made countless ones myself. Most I am not proud of, but I don't let those mistakes define or discourage me. I have learnt to find the good and the blessings in every experience.

Your learning experiences may be painful, expensive and stressful but if you learn from these experiences, you will become smarter. Your mistakes pave the way for you to succeed by revealing when you are on the wrong path.

The most significant breakthroughs come when you are feeling the most frustrated and most stuck. It is this frustration that forces you to think differently, to look outside the box and see the solution that you have been missing.

Reiterating this fact, Peter Drucker in his book Innovation and Entrepreneurship stated that the primary source of innovation in business is the unexpected success or unexpected failure. It is often the completely unanticipated event that contains the solution that you are seeking. The unexpected event that provides the answer you need can often appear to be a major setback or failure.

Success takes time and patience; you need to maintain a good attitude and have an open mind even when things seem not to be going right.

Sir Alexander Flemming in 1928 was conducting experiments in London on bacteria when some mould flew into his culture dishes and killed the bacteria. This appeared to have ruined his experiment. As he was about to throw away the culture medium and start again, he noticed the mould that had killed the bacteria.

Fleming spent several weeks growing more mould and trying to determine the particular substance in the mould that killed the bacteria. After discussing the mould with mycologist (mould expert) C. J. La Touche who had his office below Fleming's, they determined the mould to be a Penicillium mould. Fleming then called the active antibacterial agent in the mould, penicillin. This discovery won him a Nobel prize in Medicine and saved many lives during World War II.

Funny how breakthroughs come! Even when your whole life seems to have burned to the ground, from the ashes comes a new life.

Upon achieving your dream, in retrospect, you realise that every wall forced you to take an alternate path just like Flemming, which led you not only to your dream but often a far better version of your dream than you ever thought was possible. The obstacles and distractions are detours meant to redirect you to a more fabulous version of your vision.

Author of Harry Potter books J.K Rowling noted that had she really succeeded at anything else; she might never have found the determination to succeed in one arena where she truly belonged. According to her, "I was set free, because my greatest fear had been realised, and I was still alive, and I still had a daughter whom I adored, and I had an old typewriter, and a big idea. And, so rock bottom became a solid foundation on which I rebuilt my life."

Every learning experience contains the seeds of a new opportunity. Embrace them always and find the seeds within.

Overcoming Rejection

Being rejected is an opportunity for redirection. It comes to redirect you to the right tracks. It helps you to get to work. It stimulates your fighting drive. Acceptance, on the other hand, makes you relaxed. And the moment you get relaxed you are not motivated to do much anymore. You become too comfortable because you have gained the acceptance of the people you respect. Do not let this happen to you. Don't let the accolades of people get into your head. The moment you relax and stop trying hard, you will be on one spot, and gradually you will start going down. Because you can never remain in one position, it's either you are going forward, or you are going backwards. When you stop trying, you will start going backwards, and those that are working and pushing will keep going forward.

See the positive side of rejection and embrace it. See it as a good thing. We all have people in our lives who have treated us like we were not good enough or left us for the same reason, but today in retrospect you are thankful for those experiences as they have spurred you into action.

Never take rejection personal. It's always not about you, but it's about them. When you have a sense of control of your thoughts and your life it wouldn't matter at all. It will happen again and again but this timeless frequent as you go on to higher levels, but you know within you that you are good enough and you are not a finished product. You are on a journey, and you will soon arrive. Your destination is even far farther than the people who rejected you. You may be slow, but you are on your way.

Some of the people who rejected you on your way to the top most times are not able to celebrate with you at the time of your success because you have outgrown them. They will be nowhere near you. They will feel uncomfortable coming to you because the gap will be unimaginable. Trust me on this.

People that didn't acknowledge you before will be forced to recognise you when you have gotten to the place called "there".

Sometimes it sickens your heart when you are with people that don't get you. Please don't waste your time trying to explain to them or prove yourself to them. Save your breath. Quit trying to fit in. There is nothing wrong with you. They don't get you because there's more to you than meets the eye.

Sometimes when people leave you, it is God separating you from them. It may hurt at the time but later in life when you see them or hear about them; you will understand why you were not fit.

Back in secondary school, in my first year, I had some friends one in my class the others in their sophomore year who really humiliated my twin sister and me for very irrelevant reasons. We wanted so much to be their friends. They looked cool and felt superior to us. After a certain incident, they even said to us outright that we couldn't be their friends anymore. We were heartbroken. Looking back, we gave them the power to treat us that way. Also, in the first place, they were never even close to us in status in any way. And, none of them is nearly as successful or as beautiful as we are today.

Not like I am happy that those girls' lives turned out poorly, but I firmly believe God introduced the rift to separate us from their influence deliberately. We have a higher purpose and can't afford to be with people that will distract us or influence us negatively. He separates us from the group of shallow minded people and places us in associations where we will be inspired and developed. Present day, "If you don't want to be my friend, I don't want to be your friend either. The feeling is mutual." I don't give anyone power over me anymore. Neither should you.

Today, my sister and I are the young women we are today, simply because we work hard and we are continuously looking for more knowledge, opportunities and ways to make a difference not trying to fit in. We refuse to settle or be on one spot so we keep reaching for greater heights.

Some other people won't just like you for no reason at all. No matter how nice you try to be, they will still reject you. Not because they are better than you, but maybe they can't stand you, or they just can't stand your guts, or they may be jealous of you. Sometimes it is inexplicable. No matter how hard you try, it just won't work. Well, "news flash", accept that not everybody will accept you in life and you are too busy fulfilling your destiny than to worry about how to please them. If you are going to start trying to please everyone or work to make everyone who doesn't accept you to accept you, you are going to miss fulfilling your purpose in life. You cannot afford it. Move on. They don't belong in your future. God is possibly saving you from something or a situation that you aren't aware at the moment.

It may hurt now but let it go. Let it go!

Some persons, things you think that are big today will be small tomorrow

Some people you think are so "big" today, give it time, they will become small. They will be way smaller than you ever imagined tomorrow. If you keep improving yourself, you will be amazed when that happens. Have you met your primary school heroes and heroines after ten years apart; how did they look like? How about those squeaky dressed students you almost died to be their friends in your high school years. And then at the university, those students that you so wished, dreamed prayed to be their friends for one reason or the other that attracted you at the time, ten years down the line you may not want to identify with them again. It happens all over again and again throughout life. You ask yourself was I crazy? No, you were not crazy; it was what was meant for that time. You weren't any better and couldn't see any better.

Now you know who you are and you know when you work hard enough you will get to any height.

Nobody matters as much as you do. You are the most important person in every equation at every given moment.

Similarly, some things that seem essential today wouldn't be after some years. Have you noticed how new things spring up every day? The moment a new thing is unveiled it becomes obsolete as a more modern version or a different thing entirely will evolve to replace that which you consider so important.

Dealing with Criticism

Uncommon success will attract uncommon enemies and uncommon criticisms. People will come at you from different quarters. Your best friends will turn against you for no reason. You will become a topic. Count yourself lucky anyway because it's a sign of advancement. Nobody talks about losers because they are not important. You are an important personality, so you make the news.

Success comes at the price of not being one of the packs. You are different, and you are often criticised and excluded from social groups because you are different. Nevertheless being different comes with rewards like economic success and fame.

Pay no attention to the critics at all. No matter what you do, you will always have critics. They are not interested in helping you improve. They seem to enjoy watching people fail and look forward to their predictions come true. They sure do have a talent for proclaiming negative predictions. They are often jealous of people with real talent and people with the will to succeed. They sure seriously criticise those who are on the path of success. They always like playing judge, jury or God to feel relevant or appear to be above you.

This opposition often occurs because your critics aren't doing anything or not doing much. Those who are working out their dreams don't need to be threatened by your accomplishments. They are too busy to be jealous and too confident to worry about how your Success might affect them.

You must be careful of those who are doing nothing with their potential. They will be your greatest critics. Learn to expect their opposition and rise above them. Refuse to get drawn into their petty quarrels or to allow their words and actions to influence your self-esteem or your behaviour.

Every dream you share has the potential to cause jealousy so be careful with whom you share your dreams. Sometimes you must keep your dream to yourself because no other person can understand it.

Don't answer the critics. Persevere no matter what. Use their criticisms to motivate and propel you forward. You may not win the war in one battle, but you can stand firm amid each assault.

At first, they may be annoyed by you, but if you persist in your work, they become incensed. Allow the universe to fight for you.

Refuse to be intimidated by your oppressor.
Keep yourself busy and never answer your critics. Your opposers will learn that they are not as important as your goals.

Holding Onto Opportunities

If you achieve something without having prepared yourself for it in your thinking, you will not be able to hold on to it. If you make a lot of money unexpectedly, and your self-concept is not equal to it, you will be subconsciously driven to engage in behaviour to get rid of the money. This accounts for why those who win the lottery lose it within a very short while. But if you achieve success gradually, growing as a person on the inside as you increase in your productive capacity on the outside, when you finally reach the position in life that you desire, you will be ready to hold on to it indefinitely.

If you look back over your life, you will find that almost everything worthwhile that you have accomplished was preceded by what appeared to be difficulties, disappointments and temporary failures. Often you had to ride an emotional roller coaster of fear, anxiety and worry. However in retrospect, you can see that every one of those difficult experiences was essential to your becoming the kind of person you are today, and to your achieving your ultimate goal.

Step Out in Faith and Keep Moving

Your decision to take charge of your life is the seed of your success. Have the courage to step out in faith. Be proactive. Don't just sit there – do something. Try something new or different every time. Always act even when there are no guarantees of success. Keep moving. As you move forward with your desires, doors will open up to you that would not have been seen had you not been in forward motion.

The more you get exposed to, the more opportunities will come your way. Remember what we said about luck? Give yourself more to more and more and more every day. Understand that this means more challenges but your ability to persevere and overcome is what makes you the heroine.

It's hard for a person to recognise opportunities if she stays in one place. Dare to strive and experience more.

If something is not working, be willing to try different approaches. Never stay on one spot.

Success belongs to the risk takers.

14

STILL MORE THINGS TO DO

Focus on What You Want

Notice how I didn't tell you the kind of career you should embrace and the time schedule you should adopt, it's deliberate. What worked for me might not work for you, you need to know what you want and focus on that.

Be yourself always. Have the insight, courage and audacity to challenge assessments made by anyone. You don't have to be good at everything, just be good at one thing. Soon enough, you will get to the level where you will employ people to do the things you cannot do.

When you have done your best at anything, have no regrets no matter how it turns out. First position or not doesn't matter as long as you had fun in the process.

Create Your Own Blue Print

Know what you want from life and decide your own way of getting it. One of the hallmarks of discipline is your ability to become successful without being given a blueprint. Truly successful people no one tells them what to do, what time to wake up or go to work. They define it. Once at work from wherever they are, they determine their own priorities, work schedule and tasks. The self-discipline to manage their own lives well makes them different from so many people who could never survive without having someone to tell them what to do, how, why, when and where.

Success usually comes due to focus and discipline. It has very little to do with luck or happenstance. Continue to work hard. The harder and smarter you work, the luckier you will become.

Self-discipline means that you make course changes or corrections only when they will be productive in reaching your goals.

Realise that, everything worthwhile takes time. You must be willing to persevere for a long time without much evidence of progress. What you are aiming for is a fundamental long-term improvement in your life. It's taken you many years to become the person you are. You must be willing to work very hard to become someone different.

Manage Your Expectations

Whatever you expect with confidence becomes your self-fulfilling prophecy. What you get in life is not necessarily what you want but what you expect. Your expectations exert a powerful, invisible influence that causes people to behave and situations to work out as you anticipated.

Always expect the best of yourself. When you start consciously working with this mental law (expecting greater things), you will have a power for good that is virtually unlimited.

The power of positive expectations alone can change your whole personality and your life as well. When you begin to think in a positive, confident way about the main aspects of your life, you take control over what is happening to you. You begin to believe more intensely in yourself and your possibilities. You now expect more positive outcomes. You attract positive people and situations, and soon your outer life will begin to correspond to your inner world of constructive thinking.

Remember that, this entire transformation begins with your thoughts. You must create a mental equivalent of what you want to experience in your reality. Everything else will follow from that.

Once you have made a decision to do something meaningful and valuable with your life, to achieve your own ideal of personal greatness, you absolutely must go to work on changing your own mentality.

All improvement in your life begins with an improvement in your mental pictures (images). Your mental pictures (images) trigger thoughts, feelings, words and actions consistent with them. Visualisation will draw people and resources into your life to help translate your images into your realities.

If your value is that, "this is a good world" and you believe is that you are going to be successful in life, you will expect that everything that happens to you is helping you in some way. As a result, you will have a positive mental attitude toward other people, and they will respond positively toward you. You will be more cheerful and optimistic. You will be someone others want to work with and for, buy from and sell to, and generally, help to be more successful. This is why a positive mental attitude seems to go hand in hand with great success in every walk of life.

Your actions on the outside will ultimately be a reflection of your innermost values, beliefs, and expectations on the inside.

Solve Problems

Wealth comes from solving problems. When you solve a problem, not only the person you solved it for, but the universe also will reward you.

Money is a reaction to the problem solved. When you get more money, you are thrilled; you like more people, and you even like your enemies then. So, keep solving problems.

Now you will say money doesn't give happiness, probably not, but spending money will definitely make you happy. The more problems you solve, the more productive you will become and the richer you will become.

Be Solution Oriented

Always look for ways to get over, around and past the obstacles that stand in your way. Quit talking about your problems, who or what caused them. Just go ahead and ask how the challenge can be handled and then take action to deal with it.

Think solutions all the time. You will always have challenges and obstacles between you and your goals. You need to develop the ability to find solutions always in order for you to forge ahead. You can develop the skill just like any other skill. The more you focus on solutions, the more and better solutions will come to you. And, the better you get at solving problems, the more you will attract massive problems. A hero is no hero without great exploits. Xena, the Warrior Princess, wouldn't be great without tough battles. You have all it takes to overcome any challenge or obstacle in your way. You have to be realistic at all times and do what needs to be done. Your confidence and courage will see you through.

Sometimes you may not have perfect and complete self-confidence, especially when confronted with major changes or challenges but if you have been following so far, trust me, you have the know-how and skills to regain your self-confidence. Believe you can and take action. The more effort you make, the more confident you will become.

Be Observant

Always observe your surroundings. Observe the people you meet. Keep your eyes and ears open at all times. There are a lot of hidden secrets, lessons, opportunities and potentials in every encounter that may not be visible to a lot of people. But when you develop this skill, you will be amazed by what you find out.

Determine to learn new things, experience different things and meet new people every day.

Think Outside the Box

No idea is perfect no matter how good it is. There is always more than one solution to a problem. You need to keep searching and keep improving. Never get comfortable. Always find better ways. Keep asking questions and challenging processes. There is always something else you can do if your desired approach is not obtainable.

Be open to every possible idea and be willing to think outside the box. There are ideas everywhere, and if you are willing to look outside the box, you will find them.

Keep probing and be willing to try new things you will get more and more ideas.

Have Alternatives

You are as free as your options in life; hence, you must always have alternatives in every area of your life. Be it personal or business, even to the salon you use, your cream and clothes. If A doesn't work, you switch to B if C doesn't, you turn to D and so on.

Resolve to remain flexible and open no matter the circumstance you find yourself. There is always another way and a better way to accomplish anything you want. Pay attention to what it might be, find it and take action in that new direction as quickly as possible.

You are as free as the alternatives you have. The more choices you have, the greater the power you have. Develop options and alternatives continually, no matter how well things are going at the moment. The more alternatives you have in any course of action, the greater confidence you will have. You are not at the mercy of anyone or anything.

Think on Paper Always

Never trust your brain with anything. Think on paper always. Whatever idea or what you plan to do, write it down. You have to. You will get smarter and more creative by writing everything down as you progress.

Have to do lists always. In its simplest terms, to-do lists are essential for efficiency because they contain everything that you have to do — the most critical tasks at the top, the least important tasks at the bottom.

When something new comes up, you add it to the list before you do it.

Be a Canal, not a Dam

Spread wealth. Be a custodian of wealth. Be a dispenser of the universe's recourses. I hope you understand me here. The more you give, the more you will be given to give. Have the mindset of a Canal. You are a source that gives out.

Whatever you own is not for you; it is given to you to give out. It may be money, ideas, whatever it is, if you don't give it out, you won't get more. Be an encouragement to others. Help others.

Be Grateful

Wherever you find yourself celebrate that point because you've only got now, you will never be at this point again.

Gratitude for the present moment and the fullness of life now is real prosperity. As you radiate abundance, you will attract wealth to you. Live every day to the fullest.

Be grateful to God and be thankful to those that have helped you to get to this stage. No one is an island, and nobody gets to the highest peaks without the help of others. You need a host of people not just one person – mentors, spouse, kids, key employees, suppliers, associates and others.

Call your folks and thank them for the help they have rendered so far. Thank the universe always for being here at this time.

Be Creative

When you love what you do, your productivity will be high, and your specific form of creative genius will emerge.

Come up with creative ideas always. See opportunities others do not see. When one way closes, try another one. Try different ways to succeed. When you lack the funds to execute your project, find another project.

Unleash It All

The greatest crime on earth is "not developing your potential". When you develop your potentials by doing what you do best, you are helping not only yourself but the world at large. Unleash all you've got inside you before you leave this earth. Don't take any with you to the cemetery. Help make the world become a better place for you, your generation and for other generations to come.

Have a Lasting Legacy

Make your life about something more than just yourself. Share everything you have earned and learned on your journey to make a difference in the lives of as many people as possible.

Giving back is not only about giving money and gifts to the needy; find a way to give your time, energy and passion in an area that you are passionate about. Find people who are in a similar disadvantaged situation that you once were and assist them with your skills and abilities. Help them in ways they can step up from their current situation.

Cast away "me, me, and me," mentality. Always focus on the needs and interests of others. See how you can help.

Where you live or what your colour, language or culture is, does not matter. You can achieve your dreams and make a significant difference in the world.

15

CONCLUSION

Do the work that is necessary for you to reach your highest potential. I am not saying it's going to be easy, but the sacrifice will be worth the results at the end of the day.

You will spend your life wrestling with who you are and who you ought to be. You are going to face challenges from one to another before you succeed. However, you are not going to play the victim because the problems are revealing a new facet of you. The real you will emerge from these struggles.

Fully commit to achieving success. Doors have always been there, but you only see them when you fully commit.

The moment you decide to take the leap into the life of your dreams, the universe sends you everything and everybody you need at the exact time you need it.

Remind yourself that, "one step at a time" is all you need.

You never know when you are about an inch away from your lucky break. You have to do it one more time. Even if the one more time doesn't work, do it again.

Choose to love people than attack them. Don't fight the government. We depend on God not on the government. When the economy is down God gives us another source if we are ready to work.

If the people around you can't take you to the next level, kiss and say goodbye. Find new people. If you can't leave them, love them from afar. Create some distance. You can't afford any distractions. This is the perspective you should set in your life. At the right time, you will understand why and no one will tell you what to do with them.

- Never define your success with your relationships.
- Never play with people that have less to lose than you because they will destroy you.
- Never let anyone cheapen you.
- Never do anything that doesn't measure up to your worth. Refuse to do things that do not pay your desired hourly rate. Exceptions – charity works.
- Never let anyone determine what they are going to pay you, work so hard that you will be able to set the price for what you are worth. If they can't pay, you say goodbye to them.
- Never waste your time with people who are going nowhere and have no value for time.
- Never keep anything in your schedule that is no longer bearing fruit for you.
- Never spend time listening to people complaining about their problems that they don't want to do anything about.
- Never let anyone talk you into something you know is wrong.
- Never go ahead with anything you don't feel right about.
- Never let anyone intimidate you or bring you to your knees over anything. Your source is from God, not from a man, so anyone leaves or cuts the supply of anything so what? You have gotten this far; you will get ahead. You will find another way no matter what it is.
- Never give more time to critics than you would your friends.
- Never expect loyalty from someone you criticise. Each time you slam, they are closing a door until one day all the doors will be locked and there will be no access.
- Never trust your mind. Always keep a checklist for everything.

- Never stop learning. Have a knowledge map of what you want to study next, next, next and next. Be open and observant all the time. There are teachers everywhere.
- Never give up on anything. It is not over until it is over. God can send help from anywhere at any time.
- Never seize being relevant to yourself, family, and society at large. If you are not relevant, you will be discarded. If you are not a part of an equation, there's no reason to live.
- Never forget to smell the roses. Make out time to have fun.

Choose to be a success! Become inspiring!

Whatever you want to be, be the best at it and do it with excellence. Distinguish yourself with an excellent character. Make an impact and make a difference! Become inspiring in whatever you do.

Put your best into what you do and make a smack in the world. Remember there is no extra time. Whatever you do now, do it the best way the first time.

Plan for success; success is waiting for the one who plans for it and strives for it.

Deliberately strive to learn from mistakes those who have gone before you on your chosen path have made in the past. It is not because you will be able to avoid them but because you will be able to deal with them in a better way.

Guard your mind, ignore the accolades of men. Choose not to have their accolades and move higher. Always look for better ways by seeking more information and updating regularly. See what works, change what doesn't, try again and eventually you will get there.

Again, because something worked before doesn't mean it will work again. It's your job to find what works better continually.

Force yourself to take action. Get to work, step out of your comfort zone; you get results by acting. No investment means no returns! Step out the door and start your transformation journey anyway.

AFTERWORD

*D*ear Radical Being,

I couldn't conclude this book without writing this short letter to you. How are you doing? I hope you are doing great. I love you, and I want you to be the best that you can be. God loves you too and "She" wants the best for you.

We should deliberately strive to make a difference with our potentials by being relevant and contributing as much as we can. When we can't provide for ourselves, we become vulnerable. This places us in a position of weakness, but when we can take care of ourselves, we receive from a position of strength. This is the line that we should tread.

We need to fight our battles ourselves without waiting for anyone to come to the rescue. We need the skills to stand firmly on the ground in life. Some things and skills only come with experience. No school can hand them to you, and no one can prepare you for them.

We have to take charge of our lives, not leaving it to anyone. It is by taking charge of our lives that we love ourselves more and we are able to express this love outwardly as well as make our societies and the world at large a better place to live in for us and generations to come.

Please feel free to shout out to me at anytime we can talk some more. I can be reached by email on *Enakeno.Oju@Spotlightreports.com.ng* or *enakenooju@gmail.com*.

Accept my warm regards.

Enakeno Victoria Oju

CHECKLISTS

CHECKLIST A

- ✓ Define a Goal Worth Fighting For
- ✓ Plan.
- ✓ Break down your goal into bits and the processes required
- ✓ Make a daily plan that if followed will take you to your goal
- ✓ Take action - Force yourself to take action
- ✓ Cut distractions
- ✓ Prioritise the goal before anything else
- ✓ Start Anyway
- ✓ Keep at it whether you are motivated or not. Force yourself to keep moving forward
- ✓ Find role models who inspire you and learn from them. Find at least three people who have walked this road before you and follow them. Read their stories, watch their interviews. When you are done with one set find another set of three.
- ✓ Schedule occasional breaks, treats and rewards for yourself, for the strides taken. This way you don't burn out.
- ✓ No days off! Be committed every day. No skipping even for one day. Once you take a break, you've disturbed the flow.
- ✓ Keep track of your progress- measure everything you can measure
- ✓ Set monthly and weekly milestones
- ✓ Self analyse your progress
- ✓ Remove negative habits
- ✓ Keep pushing 365 days a year and repeat the next year and the next and the next
- ✓ Master discipline to remain focussed
- ✓ Have back up plans for anything that could go wrong
- ✓ Have goals all year round

CHECKLIST B

- ✓ What do you really want to do with your life?
- ✓ What stories do you want to hear people telling about you?
- ✓ How do you want people to describe you?
- ✓ How can you achieve the life of your dreams?
- ✓ What would you need?
- ✓ Who would you need in the process?
- ✓ What expertise would you require?
- ✓ Where would you go?
- ✓ Why do you want this life?
- ✓ What kind of difference would you like to make in the world?
- ✓ What legacies do you want to leave behind?

ABOUT THE AUTHOR

ENAKENO VICTORIA OJU is committed to having everyone wake up to do all it takes to possess absolute control of their destinies. Most of her works are tilted towards identifying various ways that can be used to make a difference in society as well as practical ways that can be used to address the inequalities that exist in society. She holds a B.A Degree in Theatre Arts, M.A in Media Arts, Masters in Business Administration and a PhD in Media Arts.

www.ingramcontent.com/pod-product-compliance
Lightning Source LLC
Chambersburg PA
CBHW022111090426
42743CB00008B/812